SECURITY OF ATTACHMENT AND THE SOCIAL DEVELOPMENT OF COGNITION

Security of Attachment and the Social Development of Cognition

Elizabeth Meins
Psychology Division,
Staffordshire University, UK

Psychology Press
a member of the Taylor & Francis group

Copyright © 1997 by Psychology Press Ltd
part of the Taylor & Francis group

Psychology Press Ltd., Publishers
27 Church Road
Hove
East Sussex, BN3 2FA
UK

British Library Cataloguing in Publication Data

A catalogue record for this book is available from the British Library

   ISBN 0-86377-468-7
   ISSN 0959-3977

Printed and bound in the UK by TJ International Ltd.

For Chas

Contents

Preface

The concept of infant-mother attachment has generated a vast amount of research, and in order to do full justice to all aspects of this work, I would need several volumes. The aim of this book is not to provide a comprehensive overview of attachment research, but to consider how certain aspects of the infant-mother relationship relate to development in other domains. The studies reported in the following chapters span a wide range of areas which often are not investigated with respect to children's security of attachment. Consequently, a certain amount of scene-setting has been done in moving from topic to topic in order to accommodate the varying needs of readers from different backgrounds.

As the title of the book suggests, the focus of my research is on the relationship between security of attachment and cognition. The studies which are reported thus do not consider how attachment is related to other aspects of social and emotional development, such as temperament, peer relationships or sociability. Rather, my aim is to build bridges between areas of cognitive and social developmental psychology which have traditionally been considered separately. At the outset, no particular theoretical framework seemed appropriate for integrating results from such diverse areas, but as this work has progressed, a Vygotskian approach has proved to be useful and enlightening in showing how cognitive development has its roots in social activity. In turn, this focus on the role of interpersonal interaction in the child's developing cognitive abilities has led me to consider which aspects of the caregiver's psychological makeup may be important to this process. Specifically, I discuss whether caregivers' proclivity to treat their infants as mental agents, attributing intentionality to their behaviour, may be a crucial variable.

A good many acknowledgements are in order. My first thanks go to Harry McGurk for his trust in my ability to write this book, despite having only seen me present my first ever conference paper. The research on which this book is based was funded by a PhD studentship from the Economic and Social Research Council, and I would like to thank Jim Russell for his supervision of this project and all of the mothers and children who gave up their time to take part. George Butterworth and Joan Stevenson-Hinde also deserve a mention for their guidance and encouragement, as do Alan Clarke and Peter Hobson for their useful comments, Mary Ward for teaching me how to code the strange situation procedure, and Richard Osbourne for the art work. Last, and certainly not least, a million thanks to my husband, Chas Fernyhough, without whom this book would never have been written.

CHAPTER ONE

The origins of Bowlby's attachment theory

> Throughout this enquiry my frame of reference has been that
> of psychoanalysis … Because some of my ideas are alien to
> the theoretical traditions that have become established, and
> so have met with strong criticism, I have been at pains to
> show that most of them are by no means alien to what Freud
> himself thought and wrote. On the contrary … a great
> number of the central concepts of my schema are to be found
> plainly stated by Freud. (Bowlby, 1969, p.xv)

A mother and her child are in an unfamiliar room together. The child is
about a year old and plays with some toys on the floor as the mother
reads a magazine. An unfamiliar woman enters and starts to chat to the
mother and then tries to play with the child. After a short time, the
mother gets up and leaves her child alone with this stranger. What will
the child do now? What *should* the child do now? If the mother returns
to the room after a few minutes how will the child respond? The search
for answers to these questions forms the basis of modern research into
the child's attachment to the mother (or primary caregiver)[1]. Children's
responses to being separated from and reunited with their mothers in
such "strange situations" (Ainsworth & Wittig, 1969) enable us to
establish the quality or *security* of the infant-mother attachment
relationship.

Without knowing anything about attachment theory, or developmental psychology in general, it is possible to imagine what might happen in the above scenario. Indeed, even if a person had never encountered an infant in real life, the chances are that he or she would soon offer suggestions as to what an infant would do if left alone with an unfamiliar woman. It is easy to conceive of infants doing a whole host of things in this situation: they might cry, throw a tantrum or become anxious, attempt to follow the mother out of the door or carry on as if nothing had happened, playing contentedly with the stranger. In observing infants in naturalistic settings and in this laboratory-based strange situation, researchers have witnessed all of these reactions; but taken in isolation, the infant's reactions to such a *separation* tell us remarkably little. The crucial issue for attachment research is how children react on being *reunited* with their mothers.

If we continue to rely on our intuition to predict the infant's behaviour on reunion, the gap between intuition and reality widens. The mother figure is generally regarded to be the nurturing, caring person in a child's life; children should therefore respond positively when their mothers return. However, when we observe real life reactions to this reunion, the answer is by no means this simple. Consider children who cry when their mothers leave the room: some of them will be consoled immediately by the mother's presence, others will need to be picked up and hugged before they can be comforted; but some children will cry more angrily when their mothers return and, when they are picked up to be comforted, may even strike out and stiffen or squirm in their mothers' arms. Children who attempt to follow their mothers may also react in a number of ways on reunion: they may show a desire for physical contact and closeness by approaching her or clambering onto her knee; alternatively, they may be content with merely greeting her and continuing to interact with her at a distance. Even children who seem oblivious to their mothers' leaving may surprise us in their reactions on being reunited. Some will carry on playing in much the same way, paying as little attention to the mother's return as they did to her exit, but others will immediately approach and want to be picked up.

It would seem, then, that there is nothing predictable about the behaviour of children in response to separation from and reunion with their mothers, but *patterns* in children's reactions under such circumstances can be identified. Four discrete types of infant-caregiver attachment have been defined, and I shall consider these patterns of attachment behaviour (Ainsworth, Blehar, Waters, & Wall, 1978) in more detail in the next chapter. In the mean time, the following criteria will serve to identify the four attachment groups. Those children who respond positively to their mothers on reunion—greeting, approaching, making or accepting contact with, or being comforted by her—regardless of how they reacted on separation, are described as being *securely attached*. Those children who do not seek contact or avoid their mother's gaze or physical touch are described as *insecure-avoidant*, whilst those who cannot be comforted and are overly passive or show anger towards their mothers are classified as *insecure-resistant*. Finally, children who seem to be totally disorganised and confused by the mother's return are described as *insecure-disorganised* (Main & Solomon, 1986). It is on the basis of these indices of response, observed both in the home and the research laboratory, that the concepts of the securely and insecurely attached child have evolved (Ainsworth et al., 1978). Subsequently, the notion of security of attachment has greatly enriched the field of developmental psychology, since it allows us to consider the wide spectrum of behaviours which may stem from the child's first social relationships.

The studies which will be reported in this book focus on security of attachment as assessed by the strange situation procedure, and address the consequences and correlates of a secure attachment relationship within the cognitive and linguistic developmental domains. In this chapter, I will discuss the historical beginnings of attachment theory in the work of Bowlby, charting the evolution of his theory from ethological studies and Freud's work on psychological trauma. In so doing, I wish to approach the field of attachment theory from a slightly different angle. Essentially, I will be considering security of attachment not in terms of how the child reacts to being separated from the mother (the traditional emphasis), but on how well-equipped the child is to *cope* with this separation. I shall also consider the possibility that the causes of such individual differences lie in the patterns of early dyadic interaction between infant and mother. In order to put these ideas into context, it is first necessary to consider the ideas of those who placed the child's tie to the mother at the focal point of their work: Bowlby (1958, 1969) and Freud (e.g. 1931).

BOWLBY'S THEORY OF ATTACHMENT

Regardless of whether researchers agree with his theoretical claims, John Bowlby's theory of attachment (1958, 1969) represents the starting point for research into the relationship between infant and caregiver. The theoretical emphasis of his work thus underpins, to varying degrees, virtually all subsequent work on the infant-mother attachment relationship.

The original spur for Bowlby's investigation of the tie between a mother and her child came from observations he made in his first job, working as a volunteer at a school for maladjusted children. The problems that he encountered in these children convinced him of the importance of balanced family relationships in the development of a psychologically healthy personality, and led to his decision to train as a child psychiatrist (Senn, 1977). In the 1940s, Bowlby embarked on a number of studies which investigated the adverse effects of maternal deprivation and institutional care on children's psychological well being. This background made him an obvious choice for the World Health Organisation (WHO) when they sought to commission an investigation into the mental health of children made homeless or orphaned by the Second World War. Bowlby first published his findings in a report to the WHO in 1951, in which he detailed his views on the importance of maternal care for the child's subsequent mental health. Bowlby's first exposition of a theory of infant-mother *attachment* was not, however, published until 1958.

The term *attachment* may be interpreted in any of three ways: (1) the relationship or "bond" between infant and mother; (2) the types of behaviour displayed by the infant to indicate an attachment; and (3) the more abstract psychological tie that one can feel toward a nurturing figure. Bowlby (1958) was primarily concerned with the first two interpretations, citing ethological evidence to support his claims about how human infants use certain types of behaviour to elicit *psychological* as well as physical care from their mothers. These types of behaviour in turn cement the bond between the infant and mother. In the later version of his attachment theory (Bowlby, 1969), Bowlby became increasingly influenced by ethological perspectives, and his emphasis moved toward a more explicit explanation of the *dynamics* of attachment behaviour and the attachment relationship. Before moving on to a discussion of broader issues, it is therefore worthwhile to examine how Bowlby's ideas developed over time.

Bowlby's original attachment theory (1958)

According to the original theory (Bowlby, 1958), infants demonstrate their attachments to their mothers with basic types of behaviour, such as sucking, clinging, following, crying and smiling. In this paper, Bowlby also discussed the range of psychoanalytic theories that were on offer to explain infant-mother relations. Essentially, there were four alternative theories purporting to explain the nature and origin of the infant-mother tie: (1) the theory of *secondary drive* (or "cupboard love"), which identified physiological needs for food and warmth as the reason for the child maintaining contact with the mother; (2) the theory of *primary object sucking*, which stated that infants have an innate propensity to relate first to the human breast, and then to the mother who is attached to the breast; (3) the theory of *primary object clinging*, according to which infants have an innate propensity for contact with a human being which is independent of their need for food; and (4) the theory of *primary return to womb craving*, which served to explain the infant's tie to the mother in terms of resentment at having been taken from the womb.

Of these theories, Bowlby identified most strongly with the notion of innate propensities for relating to the human breast and for contact with a human being, leading him to propose that innate drives and instinctual responses lie behind the child's desire to maintain contact with the mother. Bowlby's interest in contemporary ethological research caused him to question the theories of secondary drive and primary return to womb craving. The former theory was rejected since it was based on the premise that only physiological needs are innate; accordingly, the child's interest in and attachment to a mother figure were merely means to meet the need for food and warmth. In contrast, Bowlby argued that attachment behaviour stemmed from the primary instincts of sucking, clinging and following. His views were supported by evidence from comparative studies, which suggested that the "instinctual responses" identified by Bowlby were innate and *independent* of physiological needs. Harlow's (1961; Harlow & Harlow, 1962) classic studies of rhesus monkeys, for example, showed that when infant monkeys were given a choice of surrogate mothers, they spent the majority of their time clinging to the surrogate which offered bodily comfort, rather than one which had a feeding bottle attached. Bodily comfort therefore appeared to be of greater importance than the provision of food in the establishment of the attachment relationship. Bowlby rejected the latter theory (the notion of a desire to return to the womb) as "both redundant and biologically improbable" (1958, p.351), since it appeared to have no plausibility in terms of ontogenetic or phylogenetic survival.

As well as using ethological evidence to criticise the psychoanalytic movement's prevailing reliance on the theory of secondary drive, Bowlby cited observations of human infants to support his criticisms. He pointed out that time and again, analysts' clinical observations of infants did not tally with their reliance on the theory of secondary drive and the overriding importance of orality. For example, he cited Klein's (1957) claim that "the whole of [the child's] instinctual desires and his unconscious fantasies imbue the breast with qualities going far beyond the actual nourishment it affords" (p.5), and described Benedek (1956) as a "prisoner of orality theory" (Bowlby, 1958, p.357). Perhaps the most well-known example of such a lack of consistency is in Anna Freud's writing. Freud and Dann (1951) reported how six children had become strongly attached to one another after having lived in a concentration camp. None of these children was old enough to take on the responsibility of providing for the others, since they were all aged between three and four years, suggesting that children can develop attachments to people who do nothing to satisfy their physiological needs. Despite these findings, and other observations she made with Burlingham (Burlingham & Freud, 1942), Freud continued to support the theory of secondary drive as an explanation of infant-mother attachment. But although Bowlby rejected traditional psychoanalytic theory, he did not move completely away from Sigmund Freud's original ideas, arguing that, in contrast to later proponents of psychoanalysis, Freud himself was more open to alternative theories to explain the relationship between infant and mother. Specifically, Bowlby suggested that, at the time of his death, Freud was developing an alternative theory based on innate drives in the infant, and was therefore moving away from the theory of secondary drive.

As a final step to formulating his own theory of attachment, Bowlby considered the dynamic aspects of the infant-mother tie, again drawing on ethological data and criticising accepted psychoanalytical theory. Bowlby discussed how other species use sign-stimuli or "social releasers" to initiate social behaviour patterns such as courtship and parenting. Certain types of social behaviour are also terminated by sign-stimuli, which Bowlby suggested should be called "social suppressors". A model of this sort, whereby instinctive responses are activated by social releasers and terminated by social suppressors, appears to be a considerable advance on the prevailing psychoanalytical explanation for such phenomena. According to psychoanalytical theory, instinctive responses resulted from an accumulation of *psychic energy* (Freud, 1894), and would cease when this energy had been used up. But when this theory is applied to an example in the real world, its shortcomings soon become apparent. Consider an example used by Bowlby: a child cries when left alone in a room, but this crying immediately ceases when the child's mother returns. Using the psychic energy theory, one would have to propose that the child's cries were due to a build-up in psychic energy which was then dissipated at the time of the mother's reappearance. In contrast, we could explain the occurrence of crying as an instinctual response to regain contact with the mother, released by her exit and suppressed by her return. Compared with this account of the phenomenon, Bowlby argued that the psychoanalytical explanation was distinctly unsatisfactory.

Extending this theme, Bowlby discussed how the most common actions of the infant—smiling, gesturing to be picked up, following, crying, sucking, clinging—all serve to increase the mother's involvement with her child and can therefore be regarded as social releasers. The mother figure thus has an important role to play in establishing the attachment relationship, since she must respond to her child's cues, maintaining the dynamic system involved in the "social releaser—instinctive response—social suppressor" behaviour pattern. Bowlby summarised his theory as follows: "There matures in the early months of life of the human infant a complex and nicely balanced equipment of instinctual responses, the function of which is to ensure that he obtains parental care sufficient for his survival. To this end the equipment includes responses which promote his close proximity to a parent and responses which evoke parental activity" (ibid. p.346).

Despite the fact that Bowlby's blend of ethology and psychoanalysis represented a major improvement on anything that had previously been written on the nature of the infant-mother tie, his theory still had its shortcomings. Perhaps the two most common criticisms of Bowlby's early work were his concentration on a single attachment relationship between infant and mother, and his generalisation from *clinical* observations of children to "normal" children being reared at home. In the original theory, these two views are related to one another. Again using ethological data to back up his claims, Bowlby asserted that infants learn to centre their instinctual responses on their mother: "good mothering from any kind of woman ceases to satisfy [the infant]—only his own mother will do" (ibid. p.370). Bowlby termed this direction of instinctual responses exclusively towards the mother *monotropy*, and believed that the mother was responsible for facilitating the infant's integration into the social world. Furthermore, Bowlby argued that the mother's repeated rejection of such responses would lead to psychological damage in the child. Specifically, Bowlby said that infants incurred the worst damage if their mothers did not accept their infants' *clinging* and *following* responses. He did, however, concede that his views contradicted those of other analysts and were based on "not very systematic clinical impressions" (ibid. p.370).

Bowlby's attachment theory (1969)

These criticisms provide a clue to what is perhaps the most impressive quality of Bowlby's work: his willingness to adapt his theory in response to research findings which either supported or refuted his ideas. Bowlby was aware of the shortcomings of the original attachment theory, and in his 1969 reworking of it, he discussed in detail the great body of research on infant-mother attachment which had come to light in the intervening years, as well as elaborating on the workings of attachment behaviours and systems. For example, Schaffer and Emerson (1964) reported that one fifth of children's attachment figures did not participate even to a minor degree in any aspect of their physical care. These results thus refuted the secondary drive explanation of attachment, and confirmed Bowlby's view that attachments were not formed because infants had learnt that such people would satisfy their physiological needs. Furthermore, the children in this study were not taken from any clinical population, suggesting that the results of the study by Freud and Dann (1951), which were mentioned above, were not merely due to the severe conditions of deprivation and trauma which these children had suffered. The fact that both Schaffer and Emerson (1964) and Ainsworth (1963, 1967) reported *multiple* attachment figures in samples of normal children did, however, go against Bowlby's notion of monotropy, leading him to concede that psychologically healthy children could have more than one attachment figure.

In addition to adapting attachment theory in light of these research findings, the major addition to the later version of Bowlby's attachment theory was a more complete exposition of the *dynamics* of attachment behaviour. In the first book of his trilogy, *Attachment* (1969), *Separation* (1973) and *Loss* (1980), Bowlby explained the child's desire to remain close to the mother in terms of a *goal-corrected system*. According to this view, environmental cues played a vital role in controlling attachment behaviour, and innate responses were deemed to be of less importance.

In this later version of his theory, Bowlby once again discussed psychoanalytical doctrines and models, and a major drive behind his move to a goal-corrected systems explanation of attachment was his continued disillusionment with Freud's psychic energy model (1894). Many advances had been made in the biological sciences and in understanding the concept of feedback since the publication of his original attachment theory. Bowlby therefore felt that he could attribute purposiveness to animals without fear of being "banned from the company of respectable scientists" (1969, p.41). As a result of this new academic freedom, Bowlby argued that instinctive behaviour was governed by integrated control systems, which operated in specific environments. Instinct was therefore flexible to some extent, depending on the prevailing conditions during maturation. Among Bowlby's reasons for revising his original instinct-based theory was the increased general understanding of goal-directed behaviour and control theory. According to the new theory, the mother is arguably the most notable and interesting cue in the environment, and proximity to her becomes the child's set goal. This theory thus places less emphasis on innate instincts, and attachment behaviour is instead seen to be dependent on what occurs when the attachment systems are activated.

In other respects, the 1969 theory remained true to Freudian principles. For example, in discussing Robertson's (1952, 1953) observations of hospitalised and institutionalised children, Bowlby arrived at one of his central themes—the notion that separation from the attachment figure functions as a psychological trauma. The separations that these children had experienced in hospitals and institutions were long-term, lasting for days, weeks or months, and such separations do indeed warrant being classified as traumatic events. In observing these children, Bowlby and Robertson saw the same pattern of behaviour being repeated: first the children would *protest* at being separated from their mothers, and would not accept care from nurses or staff; next they entered a *despair* phase, during which their preoccupation with their mothers persisted, but their behaviour now betrayed feelings of increasing hopelessness and depression; finally, if separation continued, the children would pass into a *detachment* phase, where they seemed to be happier, and accepted the care and attention of others, but appeared to have lost the focus of any deep attachment.

But although this progression was consistently seen in hospitalised children, it was impossible to extrapolate these results to predict how physically well children would react to everyday separations from their mothers. Nevertheless, Bowlby's theory of infant-mother attachment depended upon the generalisability of these observations and the concept of separation as psychological trauma. Although his overgeneralisation is hardly surprising given the scarcity of observations of children in everyday contexts at that time, it is still an important example of the inveterate influence of Freudian principles on Bowlby's work. I shall return to this point later in the chapter, and offer my own suggestions as to why Bowlby chose to take this theoretical stance.

Working models

In the 1969 version of his theory, Bowlby introduced one of his most important and enduring concepts—the *working model* of the attachment figure and the self. Essentially, the working model of the attachment figure is constructed from the child's past experiences with that person—whether he or she is sensitive, available, consistent, predictable, and so on. Implicit in the concept of working models is the assumption that there will be intergenerational transfer of attachment relationships, an idea which is present in some of Bowlby's earliest theoretical work (Bowlby, 1940). The child's working model of self is constructed complementarily on the basis of "how acceptable or unacceptable he himself is in the eyes of his attachment figures" (Bowlby, 1973, p.236). The quality of interaction between the child and the attachment figure thus becomes translated into a series of mental representations which serve to provide the child with a template for future interactions with that person.

Bowlby maintained that, once formed, working models were stable, and would only change if considerable and sustained mismatches between the working model and the quality of the actual interaction were experienced, at which point the working model would accommodate to reality. If, however, this new reality represented a marked deterioration in the quality of interaction with the attachment figure, the child may resort to defensive mechanisms in order to exclude this negative information. Finally, Bowlby argued that the existence of enduring working models could explain why several researchers (e.g. Offer, 1969; Peck & Havighurst, 1960) had found that attachment patterns were transmitted from parent to child. Bowlby concluded that "the inheritance of mental health and mental ill health through the medium of family microculture... may well be more important than is their inheritance through the medium of genes" (Bowlby, 1969, p.323).

Recent evaluations

The processes involved in the establishment and alteration of working models share certain features with the concept of *resilience* in children, as discussed most recently by Fonagy, Steele, Steele, Higgitt, and Target (1994). Fonagy et al. argued that the establishment of the child's *psychological* self (in contrast to the physical self) is vulnerable, since it is dependent on children being exposed to someone who will care for them sensitively and attentively. If such care is not forthcoming, the child may adopt a defensive strategy to counter these experiences. Within the sphere of attachment, the defining characteristics of insecurity—avoidance, resistance and disorganisation—can all be seen as examples of such defence strategies. In contrast, resilient children will be able to cope with potentially more serious adverse circumstances without resorting to such defensive reactions since they have experienced a stable and nurturing relationship with their primary caregiver. Consequently, Fonagy et al. maintained that there is "a prima facie case that *resilient children are securely attached children*" (1994, p.235, original emphasis).

Even though Fonagy et al.'s argument centres on the child's ability to cope with events in the world, the concept of resilience still implies that this is coping *in the face of some traumatic event*. However, it may be that the strategies adopted in such circumstances depend on more general and pervasive features of ego development. For example, if a child's ego is sufficiently developed, separation from the attachment figure may no longer be experienced as a trauma. Such children are able to draw on their past experiences in such situations to form a framework for coping with separations. This argument echoes Bretherton's (1980) assertion that one of the most important roles of the attachment figure is to provide the child with strategies which can be used to cope with the events of everyday life. Since the essence of the secure attachment relationship is the child's trust of his or her mother, which has been established throughout infancy, securely attached children will not need to resort to defence strategies if their mothers leave them. They know that in the past their mothers have provided a secure base for them, and have been constant, stable and consistent. Thus, although the securely attached child may cry when his or her mother leaves, such a separation does not cause the child psychological trauma, which is why no defence behaviours are seen on the child's subsequent reunion with the mother. It was for similar reasons that I said that the child's reaction to reunion, rather than separation, was the crucial issue in attachment (p.2).

If the establishment of a secure attachment relationship is also the nurturing of the ego, this may explain why wide-ranging advantages have been observed in securely attached infants as they grow up (see Chapter Two for a full discussion of this literature). Just as it has been demonstrated that a confiding relationship in adulthood protects against depression after a life event (e.g. Brown & Harris, 1978), so certain factors associated with a secure infant-mother attachment may help the child to cope first with the distress of being separated from the attachment figure, and later with a range of everyday challenges. Rather than viewing the relation between ego strength and security of attachment as simply one of cause and effect, I would argue that it is the *precursors* of a strong sense of ego and a secure attachment which are the same, or at least similar. Before outlining the theoretical framework which leads me to make such a claim, the place of the ego within Bowlby's theory needs to be discussed.

FREUD'S INFLUENCE ON BOWLBY

Although Bowlby was critical of psychoanalytical theory and its proponents, in the 1969 version of his theory he continued to identify strongly with Freud's writing, and to illustrate that his views were consistent with those of Freud. Building on his earlier ideas, Bowlby (1969) considered in greater depth the alternative perspectives that Freud (1939, 1940) had outlined relating to psychological trauma. Freud presented two alternative interpretations, in terms of: (1) the nature of the event *per se*; or (2) the individual characteristics which will affect one's reaction to the event. Bowlby described Freud's position as follows:

When an experience evokes unusual pathological reaction, Freud argues, the reason is that it makes excessive demands on the personality... by exposing the personality to quantities of excitation greater than it can deal with. As regards constitutional factors, Freud supposes that individuals must vary in the extent to which they can meet such demands, so that 'something acts as a trauma in the case of one constitution but in the case of another would have no such effect' (S.E., 23, p.73). At the same time, he holds, there is a particular phase of life, the first five or six years, during which every human being tends to be vulnerable. The reason for this ... is that at that age 'the ego ... is feeble, immature and incapable of resistance'. In consequence, the ego 'fails to deal with tasks which it could cope with later on with utmost ease', and instead resorts to repression or splitting (ibid., p.10).

This shows that Bowlby was certainly aware of Freud's views on the role played by the ego in coping with psychological trauma. The problem was whether separation from one's mother could be viewed within the context of the protective effect of the ego. Bowlby was uncertain whether Freud would have sanctioned such a view, noting that "although there is no doubt that early separation can injure the ego, whether this was Freud's view is uncertain" (ibid. pp.11-12). There was, however, no such uncertainty in identifying early separation from the mother with Freud's definition of a traumatic event. Consequently, Bowlby became interested in the infant's separation from the mother in terms of the associated trauma, instead of the role played by the ego, and defined separation as a "pathogen". Thus, in the absence of other differentiating characteristics, all children should react in the same way.

Psychoanalytical dogma

Why was Bowlby so obviously concerned about his theory being consistent with Freud's ideas? The answer to this question may be found in the response of the psychoanalytical movement to Bowlby's three seminal papers: *The nature of the child's tie to his mother* (1958); *Separation anxiety* (1960a); and *Grief and mourning in infancy and early childhood* (1960b). As we have seen, in dealing with the three themes—attachment, separation and loss—on which his life's work was based, Bowlby drew on evidence from a number of disciplines outside the field of psychoanalysis. The members of the British Psychoanalytic Society found his eclectic approach not merely controversial, but heretical. "Bowlby? Give me Barrabas" was the reaction of one of its members (Grosskurth, 1987). More importantly, influential analysts such as Anna Freud and Schur were open in their condemnation of Bowlby's revisionist theory, and Spitz (1960) stated that Bowlby's ideas "becloud the observational facts, are oversimplified, and make no contribution to the better understanding of observed phenomena" (p.93). In the face of such criticism, it is little wonder that in his subsequent reworkings of attachment theory, Bowlby went to such lengths to reassure his readers that the ideas were consistent with Freudian principles, and, when two alternative theoretical pathways were presented, chose that which was most congruent with Freud's writings.

While such dogmatic views do not prevail today, it is still worthwhile to follow Bowlby's lead and clarify how the theoretical approach I shall adopt here tallies with orthodox attachment theory. I have already indicated my preference for understanding the child's reaction to separation from the mother figure in terms of the ego's ability to cope with such an event. In doing so, we can move away from Bowlby's assumption that separation from mother is a traumatic event for the child. There is, however, a further point of divergence between the views expressed here and those of Bowlby and Freud, with regard to the *timing* of the development of the attachment relationship and the ego. Freud asserted that the most important time for ego development was between the ages of two and four, and was uncertain of the significance of the early months of life. Bowlby (1969) was willing to admit that an attachment can begin to form before this time, but the earliest age he identified was six months. In contrast to both of these views, the Soviet psychologist Lev Vygotsky (1978) held that development in all areas begins *from the first days of life*, and it is Vygotsky's ideas which provide the theoretical framework for my approach to attachment.

Although at first sight this may seem an odd alliance, there are a number of reasons for proposing a Vygotskian framework for attachment research. Firstly, Vygotsky stressed the importance of interpersonal interaction in the development of the higher mental functions. For example, his "general genetic law of cultural development" states, "any function in the child's cultural development appears twice, or on two planes. First it appears on the social plane and then on the psychological plane. First it appears between people as an interpsychological category, and then within the child as an intrapsychological category ... Social relations or relations among people genetically underlie all higher functions and their relationships" (1981, p.163). Since the attachment to the primary caregiver is the first social relationship the child will form, it will clearly be of major importance in cognitive development.

Vygotsky's general genetic law of cultural development also highlights a number of other common features of the two approaches. This law can help us to understand Bowlby's concept of working models of attachment figures and the self which the child mentally constructs on the basis of past experience with such people. Indeed, the internalisation process which Vygotsky proposed may provide us with the mechanism by which the child acquires these working models. Of course, the most obvious connection between them is in their focus on the *dynamics* of the relationship, rather than the individual traits of either mother or child. The emphasis on the attachment relationship is thus consistent with Vygotsky's notion of the *dyad* as the most suitable unit of analysis for development.

As Bretherton (1987) noted, this Vygotskian framework for understanding attachment may even find echoes in Bowlby's early work. For example, in the following extract, Bowlby discusses his views on how, in nurturing the child's ego and super-ego, the mother enables the child to acquire self-regulatory behaviour:

It is not surprising that during infancy and early childhood these functions are either not operating at all or are doing so most imperfectly. During this phase of life, the child is therefore dependent on his mother performing them for him. She orients him in space and time, provides his environment, permits the satisfaction of some impulses, restricts others. She is his ego and his super-ego. Gradually he learns these arts himself, and as he does, the skilled parent transfers the roles to him ... Ego and super-ego development are thus inextricably bound up with the child's primary human relationships (Bowlby, 1951, p.53).

This passage provides an ideal example of the infant-mother dyad functioning within what Vygotsky (1978) termed the *zone of proximal development* (ZPD).

My central argument will be that this type of sensitive, contingent interaction during the first months of life nurtures both the child's security of attachment and the ability to function in an autonomous and independent fashion. A Vygotskian approach to attachment represents a largely unexplored opportunity for bridging the gap between the socioaffective and cognitive domains, and the measure of its usefulness will be its ability to explain the differences observed between securely and insecurely attached children as they develop. Before moving on to the experimental studies which form the main content of this book, it is necessary to discuss the security-based differences that we already know to exist, and the experimental procedures for assessing children's attachments to their primary caregivers.

NOTE

1. In line with the vast majority of studies in this area, my research focuses exclusively on the child's attachment to the mother as the primary caregiver. In more recent years, an interesting line of research has opened into children's attachments to other caregivers (most notably fathers), and how family structures in different cultures and in non-traditional settings might alter the balance of attachment relationships (e.g. Lamb, 1981; Sagi et al., 1995). In what follows, the reader should bear in mind two points: first, that my use of the terms "mother" and "caregiver" is interchangeable; and second, that the term "mother" is not necessarily restricted to the child's biological mother.

CHAPTER TWO

Security of attachment: Correlates and consequences

> Today we know that the central task of developmental psychiatry is to study the endless interaction of internal and external and how the one is constantly influencing the other, not only during childhood but during adolescence and adult life as well. (Bowlby, 1988, p.1)

In the period between Bowlby's original and revised theories of attachment (1958, 1969), a number of researchers set about the task of observing how infants express their attachments in real-life contexts. The most influential of these researchers was Mary Ainsworth. While Bowlby's primary concern remained the making and breaking of attachments, Ainsworth's approach has been more qualitative. Indeed, her biggest contribution to this field remains the identification and description of the *patterns* of attachment, and the development of a technique by which they could be measured.

AINSWORTH'S EARLY OBSERVATIONAL STUDIES

Ainsworth worked with Bowlby in London during the early 1950s, at which time she became involved with Bowlby and Robertson's collaborative project on the long-term effects of early separation from the attachment figure. In reading the reports on these children,

Ainsworth was struck by a number of patterns in their behaviour and psychological makeup which she believed to be related to their early experiences.

Ainsworth went on to apply her working knowledge of child behaviour to her early studies on infant-mother interaction in Uganda (Ainsworth, 1963, 1967), which represent the first documented evidence for Bowlby's goal-corrected systems of attachment (see p.8 of this book). Over the seven months that Ainsworth observed these women and children, a vast amount of data were collected on infants' responses to their mothers' behaviour and to the presence of other adults who were frequent visitors to their homes. Ainsworth's measure of attachment was based on the infant's demonstration that he or she discriminated the mother from other people and responded to her in a different way. Such a discrimination could be shown by the infants' responses toward the mother. For example, infants would cry when someone other than the mother held them or when the mother left the room; greeting, following and orienting towards the mother were also ways in which infants showed that they distinguished their mothers from other familiar adults. Ainsworth found considerable variation from one family to the next, both in terms of the frequency and strength of attachment behaviours, and in the way infants organised their responses with respect to maternal behaviour. The speed at which infants formed an attachment varied greatly; one infant demonstrated differential crying at 8 weeks, another regularly cried when the mother left the room at 15 weeks, whereas other infants were still not showing an obvious attachment at 12 months.

The experience of working on Bowlby and Robertson's project, and the observations she made while living among the Ganda people in Uganda, were of great importance in shaping Ainsworth's theoretical and methodological approach to infant-mother attachment. Theoretically, her research has concentrated on *individual differences* in the attachment relationship, why they occurred and their impact on the child's subsequent development. Methodologically, Ainsworth favours detailed observations as the basis for assessing these individual differences. On her return to the United States, Ainsworth set about establishing whether the patterns of interaction she had observed in the Ganda were typical of American infants and mothers. From the results of her studies in Baltimore, Ainsworth constructed a laboratory-based observational procedure for assessing patterns of attachment; this procedure was to revolutionise research into the infant-caregiver attachment relationship.

The strange situation

Although it was apparent from Bowlby's work that observing children during long-term separations from their mothers did not provide a prototypical profile of how a child would react to "normal" separations, investigating attachment behaviour by observing children and their mothers solely in the home environment also appeared to have its limitations. It could be argued that the demonstration of strong attachment behaviour in the home (e.g. crying loudly, clinging to the mother if she attempts to leave the room) may be an indication of a *less* than optimal attachment relationship. The strange situation procedure (Ainsworth & Wittig, 1969) was developed to provide an alternative means of assessing the attachment relationship. Although this procedure is a brief, structured laboratory test, it was based on the very precise and thorough home-based observations made by Ainsworth in Uganda and Baltimore (Ainsworth, 1963, 1967; Ainsworth, Bell, & Stayton, 1971). From these data, Ainsworth identified the types of events which were important indicators of the quality of the attachment relationship, and this vast body of data was distilled into the individual episodes of the strange situation procedure. Specifically, Ainsworth maintained that infants' responses to separations and reunions were particularly enlightening about the quality of the attachment relationship, which meant that the strange situation procedure was relatively easy to construct (Ainsworth, 1995).

As Table 2.1 shows, the order of events in the strange situation is designed first to elicit exploratory behaviour and then, through a series of mildly stressful events, to shift the infant's attention to seeking proximity to and maintaining contact with the mother. The coding procedure for the strange situation was developed by Ainsworth, Blehar, Waters, and Wall (1978), and focused on four different categories of behaviour: proximity seeking, contact maintenance, avoidance and resistance. Ainsworth's work made it possible to grade an infant's attachment to the mother much more precisely than had previously been possible, and thus the concept of *security* of attachment was born. From this point onwards in attachment research, the major concern was not whether an infant had formed an attachment (since all infants will do so if an attachment figure is available), but whether the resulting attachment relationship was secure.

The proximity-seeking and contact-maintenance indices of behaviour are typical of securely attached children upon reunion with their mothers. High scores on the two remaining indices—avoidance and resistance—are indicative of an insecure attachment. Ainsworth et al. (1978) identified two types of insecurity: (1) an insecure-avoidant or type A attachment; and (2) an insecure-resistant or type C attachment. Type

TABLE 2.1
Ainsworth and Wittig's (1969) strange situation procedure

1.	Mother and baby introduced into room
2.	Mother and baby alone, baby free to explore (3 minutes)
3.	Stranger enters, sits down, talks to mother and then tries to engage the baby in play (3 minutes)
4.	Mother leaves. Stranger and baby alone (up to 3 minutes*)
5.	First reunion. Mother returns and stranger leaves unobtrusively. Mother settles baby if necessary, and tries to withdraw to her chair (3 minutes)
6.	Mother leaves. Baby alone (up to 3 minutes*)
7.	Stranger returns and tries to settle the baby if necessary, and then withdraw to her chair (up to 3 minutes*)
8.	Second reunion. Mother returns and stranger leaves unobtrusively. Mother settles baby and tries to withdraw to her chair (3 minutes)

*If the mother feels that her child is becoming overly upset, these episodes may be terminated before the full three minutes has elapsed.

A attachment has subsequently been shown to relate to maternal rejection during the last quarter of the first year of life (e.g. Ainsworth, 1982; Isabella, 1993); avoidant children turn their attention to the environment, perhaps because they have learnt that nurturance will not be forthcoming from their mothers. The type C pattern of attachment has recently been associated with inconsistent mothering over the first year (e.g. Isabella, 1993; Isabella & Belsky, 1991); the resistant child appears unable to disengage from the mother, reacting with anger, ambivalence or passivity to her unpredictability. A secure attachment represents a balance between over-involvement with the environment or with the mother, and is labelled type B (see Fig. 2.1). In the pre-separation episodes, securely attached children will typically explore the environment, but as the strange situation proceeds, their balance of behaviour will increasingly tip toward proximity-seeking and contact-maintaining behaviour. In contrast, insecurely attached children tend not to show the same balance between exploration and attachment.

In addition to these three attachment categories, a number of subtypes have been identified. The two insecure categories are each divided into two. A1 infants demonstrate the most conspicuous avoidance, whereas A2 infants show some attempts at approach, although they are typically abandoned before the mother is reached. C1 infants show high levels of overt resistance, with angry crying and tantrum-like behaviour, in contrast to the passivity and covert resistance of infants in the C2 category. The secure category includes

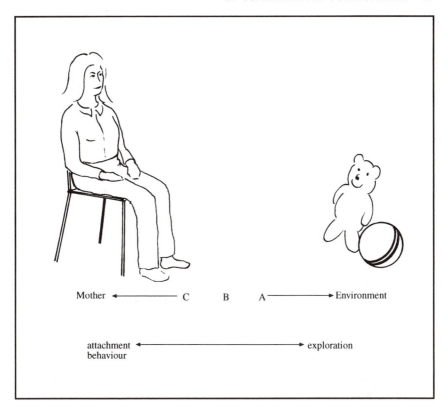

Mother ◄——————— C   B   A ——————► Environment

attachment ◄——————————————► exploration
behaviour

FIG. 2.1. Attachment as a balance of behaviour directed toward mother and the environment.

four subtypes. B1 infants tend to show little distress on separation and do not appear to need physical contact on reunion; however, they can be distinguished from the avoidant category by their willingness to greet their mothers and establish contact through "interaction at a distance". B2 infants resemble the B1 group, but are more likely to seek physical contact with the mother, especially in episode 8 (see Table 2.1). B3 infants are the most securely attached of all, actively seeking contact with their mothers, and maintaining it once achieved. B4 infants appear to be completely preoccupied with their mothers throughout the strange situation, and become extremely upset during the separation episodes. Although these infants tend to show some resistance, they can be distinguished from group C by their strong proximity seeking and capacity to be comforted by their mothers. The three attachment categories can thus be seen to represent a continuous spectrum of behaviour from conspicuous avoidance to conspicuous resistance. In addition to the original ABC attachment categories, Main and Solomon

(1986) established the D category for those infants whose behaviour was difficult to classify using the original system. These infants demonstrate no obvious pattern in their responses to their mothers on reunion; they appear disoriented and anxious and their behaviour is disorganised. Children who receive a primary classification of type D are, however, also given a secondary, "forced" classification using Ainsworth et al.'s (1978) three original attachment categories.

The classifications obtained in the strange situation have been found to have concurrent and predictive validity (e.g. Ainsworth et al., 1978; Waters & Sroufe, 1983), and several authors (e.g. Main & Weston, 1982; Vaughn, Egeland, Sroufe, & Waters, 1979) have shown that they are stable over the late infancy period. These findings led Vaughn, Deane, and Waters (1985) to conclude that the strange situation procedure "has become de facto *the* attachment situation" (p.112, original emphasis). But although the strange situation has proved to be a reliable and valid measure of security of attachment, it does have its limitations. For example, its method and scoring procedures are only suitable for infants in a small age range and cannot be applied without modification to children older than about two years. Moreover, because the strange situation is a controlled, laboratory-based procedure, it is difficult to use in studies which are not based in institutions. Because of these limitations, researchers began to focus on the concept of *secure base* behaviour in an attempt to devise a more flexible alternative procedure for assessing the attachment relationship.

THE SECURE BASE

One of the main characteristics of securely attached children is their ability to use the mother as a "secure base" from which to explore the world: in their exploration of the environment, they constantly use their mothers as a reference point. Their explorations are thus interactive and social processes rather than individual endeavours. In fact, Ainsworth (1973) argued that secure base behaviour was a better indicator of a secure attachment than the occurrence of basic attachment behaviours, since these behaviours were context-dependent. For example, Ainsworth found that crying *per se* was not a particularly accurate index of security, and children who cried and fussed most frequently were more likely to be insecurely attached. Crying was only a good index of security of attachment if it occurred in response to a stressful event, such as the attachment figure leaving. Ainsworth thus viewed individual differences in infant attachment as "qualitative differences in the way attachment behaviors are organized, rather than as differences in the strength of some generalized drive or trait" (Ainsworth, 1972, p.124). This notion of attachment as an organisational construct has been adopted by many researchers in the attachment field, most notably Sroufe and Waters (1977).

Secure base behaviour is characterised by the child returning to the mother before venturing out for the next exploration, perhaps bringing her a toy, or attracting her attention with a vocalisation. Even if securely attached children do not physically return to their mothers, they will often use visual referencing to punctuate their exploration. If the mother takes up these cues, she can become involved in the child's developing understanding of the world. Such children are thereby afforded a degree of autonomy and independence, and allowed to explore their immediate environment, knowing that their mothers will be available for support and comfort if it is needed. This knowledge is not something that is instinctual; rather, it is based on the child's past experiences and the mother's demonstration of her availability and nurturance over a long period of time.

As a means of quantifying differences in secure base behaviour so that they could be utilised in an assessment of security, Waters and Deane (1985) developed the Attachment Q-Sort (AQS). The original AQS contained 100 items describing various types of behaviour which were indicative of or related to attachment. In the revised version (Waters, 1987) the number of items is reduced to 90 behaviours which betray the child's use of the attachment figure as a secure base. Each of these items is written onto a card, and the child's classification is obtained by these cards being sorted into different piles, ranging from behaviours most characteristic of the child to those which are least characteristic. These piles are then adjusted to provide a symmetrical, unimodal distribution of items which makes up the final sort. Children's Q-sort profiles thus indicate to what extent secure base behaviour is a typical feature of their interaction with their attachment figures. The advantages of the AQS are that it can be used in any situation, is applicable to children up to five years of age and can be administered by a wide variety of people. For instance, several studies have used the mother as the rater of the AQS, and cross-cultural studies have shown that women from severely deprived backgrounds are quite capable of administering this procedure adequately (e.g. Posada et al., 1995). The AQS thus represents a useful alternative to the strange situation procedure for measuring security of attachment.

Clearly, a number of factors will affect the establishment of a secure attachment relationship and the child's ability to use the mother as a secure base. Certain traits of the mother and infant must be compatible if an efficient system of interaction and exchange is to evolve, and perhaps the largest area of attachment research has focused on this issue.

CORRELATES OF SECURITY OF ATTACHMENT

Several studies have identified certain maternal characteristics which are associated with a secure infant-mother attachment. Ainsworth, Bell, and Stayton (1971) found that mothers of securely attached children were more sensitive, accepting, cooperative and accessible to their infants' requests than mothers in the avoidant and resistant insecure groups. There were also distinguishing features of the mothers in the two insecure attachment groups: mothers of avoidant children were more rejecting than those of resistant children, and expressed aversion to close bodily contact consistently more than other mothers. Ainsworth et al. noted that the mother of a securely attached child was "capable of perceiving things from [the child's] point of view" and seemed to respect the child "as a separate person; she also respects his activity-in-progress and thus avoids interrupting him" (1971, p.43).

Tracy and Ainsworth (1981) looked at ways in which a mother shows affection for her child. Their results showed that mothers of securely attached children were more likely to show affection by hugging or cuddling (rather than kissing or stroking) their children. Hugging and cuddling were particularly rare amongst the mothers in the insecure-avoidant group, although these mothers were much more likely to kiss their children than those in both the secure and insecure-resistant groups. Perhaps the most interesting finding of this study was that these variations between the mothers in the three attachment groups were *qualitative* rather than quantitative, since no difference was found between the groups with regard to the frequency of affectionate acts. The problem was not that rejecting mothers did not feel love or affection for their babies, but that their feelings of irritation, resentment and even anger tended to restrict their ability to show their positive emotions physically. Tracy and Ainsworth used this anomaly in these mothers' behaviour to explain their insecure-avoidant infants' reactions in the strange situation: even though the attachment system is activated, resulting in a need for bodily contact, previous disappointments upon being rejected seem to prevent these children from seeking comfort in this way.

Egeland and Farber (1984) identified certain personality factors in the mothers of children in the secure and insecure groups which may account for their different patterns of caregiving. Mothers of securely attached babies were responsive to their infants' cries, had positive views about themselves and their babies, and were more skilled in feeding and playing. Mothers of insecure-avoidant children tended to be tense, irritable and lacking in confidence, reacting negatively to motherhood and handling their babies as little as possible. In addition, mothers of insecure-resistant children were found to have lower IQs, and their babies were less alert and did not appear to seek responsive interaction with their mothers. Egeland and Farber suggested that this lack of social engagement in insecure-resistant babies may be in part responsible for the inconsistent patterns of caregiving found in their mothers.

Factors relating to type D (insecure-disorganised) attachment

The correspondence between maternal sensitivity and the quality of infant-mother interaction extends to the extreme case of infants who fall into the D category. Although a type D attachment classification can arise in "normal" samples, there is a growing body of evidence linking this type of insecure attachment to abuse (Carlson, Cicchetti, Barnett, & Braunwald, 1989) and maternal depression (Radke-Yarrow et al., 1995).

Carlson et al. (1989) compared the distribution of attachment classifications from a group of maltreated infants with those of a control group matched for social stressors such as poverty and poor housing. The maltreatment group had been identified by social services as in need of intervention because of child abuse or neglect. Of the maltreating mothers, 23% had physically injured the child, 69% had emotionally mistreated the child and 82% were guilty of neglect. Carlson et al. found that the vast majority of the children in the maltreatment group fell into category D (18 out of 22 children), with only three children being classified as securely attached. In comparison, over half of the children in the control group were securely attached (11 out of 21) and only four fell into category D. From these results, Carlson et al. argued that the insecure-disorganised classification in the strange situation should be used diagnostically to identify children who are at risk.

Radke-Yarrow et al. (1995) reported a similar skew towards the insecure-disorganised category in children of depressed mothers, particularly those whose mothers suffered from bipolar depression. They found that 16% of control group children showed disorganised patterns of attachment, compared with 23% of children whose mothers were unipolarly depressed and 42% in the bipolar depression group.

It seems obvious that emotional expression during interaction will be affected if a mother is depressed. A depressed mother will be less likely to smile at her child and may be psychologically unavailable, which would make reciprocal communicative exchanges briefer and less frequent. But there is also evidence that the *content* of the mother's speech alters if she is suffering from depression. Murray and Stein (1989) found that depressed mothers talked to their babies using more self-oriented, critical and controlling speech than a group of non-depressed mothers. This style of interaction between the mother and infant at three months was found to be related to the child's performance on an object permanence task at nine months of age. Infants succeeded on the task if their mother's speech during the interaction at three months had focused on the infant's actions and experiences, but failed if maternal speech had been mother-centred. Such differences in the patterns of early interaction and communication may thus even affect the infant's ability to perform a cognitive task. The infant and mother characteristics which are associated with the four attachment categories are summarised in Table 2.2.

TABLE 2.2
The characteristics associated with the four attachment classifications

Attachment classification	*Associated characteristics*
Type A (insecure-avoidant)	Infants do not show distress on separation from, and avoid closeness and contact on reunion with, attachment figure. Their mothers show affection by kissing, but express an aversion to close bodily contact. These mothers may also be psychologically unavailable and thus fail to meet their infants' desires.
Type B (secure)	Infants use their attachment figure as a secure base from which to explore the world. On reunion with their attachment figure these infants show no avoidance or resistance. Their mothers are more sensitive and cooperative, and are also aware of, and show respect for, their infants' desires.
Type C (insecure-resistant)	Infants show considerable distress on separation from their attachment figure, crying angrily or throwing a tantrum. These infants cannot be comforted by contact with their attachment figure and continue to show resistance upon reunion. Alternatively, these infants may be very passive. Their mothers tend to be of lower IQ, and are inconsistent in their patterns of mothering.
Type D (insecure-disorganised)	Infants show no set pattern of behaviour on separation from, or reunion with, their attachment figure. Their response to reunion may be contradictory, e.g. strong proximity-seeking coupled with strong avoidance. Alternatively, they may show fearful, stereotypical or odd behaviours when their attachment figure returns. Type D attachment is more common in infants who have been abused or whose mothers have suffered from depression.

THE CONSEQUENCES OF SECURITY
OF ATTACHMENT

If mothers of securely attached children provide appropriate environmental support both in everyday interactions and novel situations, does this result in these children having a relatively strong sense of their own efficacy as human agents? There is evidence which points to infants' security of attachment affecting their subsequent development in a number of areas.

Task completion and problem solving

The results of a number of studies suggest that infantile security of attachment is related to children's ability to engage in and solve cognitive tasks in early childhood. Matas, Arend, and Sroufe (1978) reported security-based differences in children's performance in completing a series of puzzles at age 2. The securely attached children were more successful than their insecurely attached peers because they were more enthusiastic, compliant to instructions, positive in affect, persistent and attentive. These findings have been replicated by Gove (1983) and Frankel and Bates (1990). Frankel and Bates reported that securely attached 2-year-olds were better than their insecure peers at solving problems which required them to join two sticks together in order to remove a toy from a long tube, or to weigh down one end of a see-saw enclosed within a glass box to reach the biscuit on the opposite end. Securely attached toddlers have also been found to be more independent explorers of their environment, and are more innovative in their ability to solve spatial problems (Hazen & Durrett, 1982) .

Symbolic play

Research into the relationship between security of attachment and symbolic play will be discussed in greater detail in Chapter Five, but a number of findings are worthy of note here. In infancy, securely attached children have been found to engage in more frequent and sophisticated sequences of pretence than their insecurely attached peers (Belsky, Garduque, & Hrncir, 1984; Bretherton, Bates, Benigni, Camaioni, & Volterra, 1979; Matas et al., 1978). In early childhood, there no longer appear to be security-based differences in children's capacity for symbolic play, but securely attached children are more likely to organise their play around a theme, and, unlike that of the insecure children, their play is enhanced by maternal involvement (Slade, 1987a).

Autonomy and independence

Sroufe, Fox, and Pancake (1983) found that children who had insecure attachments in infancy were rated by their teachers as being significantly more dependent than their securely attached peers. The insecurely attached children were more likely to seek help in self and social management, and spent more time in close proximity to their teachers or sitting on the teacher's lap. These findings were supported and extended by Turner (1993). She observed that not only did insecurely attached children demonstrate more dependent behaviour during free play, but their requests for help were significantly less likely to elicit adult compliance than similar bids from securely attached children. It would appear that the adults viewed the requests made by children in the secure group as being somehow more "genuine" because they were appropriate to the situation, or arose when these children were incapable of managing alone. These differences may be due to the way in which securely attached children approach interactions with others. Lütkenhaus, Grossmann, and Grossmann (1985) reported that 3-year-olds who had been classified as securely attached in infancy interacted more quickly and smoothly with an experimenter. This assessment of interaction was made on the basis of children's initial reactions to an experimenter entering their home. The securely attached children tended to approach the experimenter without hesitation and talked to him without being asked to do so, whereas the insecure children were more likely to hide from the experimenter, cry or cling to their mothers. These results are consistent with those of Main and Weston (1981) who found that, in a non-stressful situation with one of their parents present, securely attached children were more sociable with a clown who attempted to engage the infant in various games. In contrast, the insecurely attached children were more likely to show "conflict" behaviour, such as engaging in disordered activity or inappropriate affect.

Persistence and "ego strength"

Ego strength can be defined as a robust sense of selfhood which spurs the individual to be persistent and to try harder when faced with possible failure. The security-based differences discussed above may thus be due to differences in ego strength, and there is direct evidence that security of attachment and ego strength are related. For example, Lütkenhaus et al. (1985) showed that 3-year-olds who had been classified as securely attached at 12 months were likely to improve their performance when they saw themselves losing a competitive game. The goal of the game was to build a tower of ten rings by stacking them on a peg, and trials were fixed so that the child always won the first time, after which wins and losses were alternated on successive trials. Lütkenhaus et al. reported that securely attached children seemed to muster every available resource in an attempt to avert failure, in contrast to the response of their insecurely attached peers, who were more likely to give up. These authors argued that the behaviour of the securely attached children was indicative of greater ego strength.

Ego strength can also be expressed in terms of the child's interaction with peers. Lieberman (1977) found that a secure attachment relationship was associated with peer competence, as measured by the child's ability to deal flexibly with a situation by exchanging information with others (Bruner, 1974). Similarly, Waters, Wippman, and Sroufe (1979) found that 3-year-olds who had been secure in their attachments as infants scored significantly higher on scales measuring peer competence and ego strength.

Ego strength is closely related to the concept of ego resilience (Block & Block, 1980), which is defined as the capacity to react in a flexible, persistent and resourceful manner, particularly in problem situations. Arend, Gove, and Sroufe (1979) reported that teachers of 4 to 5-year olds who had been classified as securely attached in infancy rated them more highly on scales of ego resilience than their insecurely attached peers. The securely attached children also demonstrated higher levels of ego resilience in a laboratory-based session, in which they had to perform a number of tasks. Taken together, these findings relating to the greater ego strength and resilience of securely attached children may account for their higher levels of self-esteem in early childhood (Sroufe, 1983).

ALTERNATIVE EXPLANATIONS

From the evidence discussed so far, the emerging characteristics of the securely attached child seem to be independence, self-effectiveness and autonomy. But could these differences be caused by other factors which are unrelated to the security of the attachment relationship? The most obvious explanation for securely attached children's superior performance on the range of tasks discussed above is that securely attached children are simply brighter than their insecurely attached peers. This explanation is not, however, supported by the literature. In a recent meta-analysis of 25 studies which had included measures of both attachment and general cognitive ability, van IJzendoorn, Dijkstra, and Bus (1995) reported that the association between these measures was small, and in fact only two of the studies found a relationship between cognitive ability and security of attachment (Main, 1983; Matas et al., 1978). Indeed, van IJzendoorn et al. concluded that "for all practical purposes the association between attachment and IQ is too weak to recommend the routine inclusion of IQ tests in order to control for this type of cognitive difference" (p.125). The advantages that securely attached children enjoy therefore appear to be a reflection of their ability to engage in and persist with a task, and are *independent* of general cognitive capacity.

The external environment

There are various disparities in living and child-rearing circumstances which could arguably account for the observed differences between secure and insecure children. Lamb et al. (1984), in one of the first critiques of the attachment literature, argued that a child's security of attachment is only a good predictor of subsequent development if home circumstances remain stable. Research on the effects of the external environment on the child's attachment behaviour has focused on two major areas: cross-cultural differences, and the role played by non-maternal care. Findings in both of these areas have been somewhat contradictory, however, which makes it difficult to arrive at any firm conclusions about the role played by culture and daycare in children's patterns of attachment.

Early cross-cultural studies suggested that there were marked differences in the distribution of infants' attachment classifications between countries. On the basis of American studies, the standard distribution (excluding type D) approximates to 70% securely attached, 20% insecure-avoidant and 10% insecure-resistant. In contrast to this split across the categories, Grossmann, Grossmann, Huber, and Wartner (1981) reported that 52% of their German sample were insecure-avoidant, with only 35% being classified as securely attached. The converse skew in distribution was reported in a Japanese sample by Miyake, Chen, and Campos (1985), who found that 37% of these infants showed the insecure-resistant pattern of attachment, and none fell into the avoidant category.

These cross-cultural differences are interesting for a number of reasons, the most important of which is that they show that the strange situation procedure is not a culturally-independent tool for assessing the quality of the attachment relationship. There are cultural differences in child-rearing practices which may lead to these skews in distribution in non-American samples, and we must therefore be cautious in interpreting strange situation behaviours as indicative of security of attachment in other cultures. For example, Grossmann, Grossmann, Spangler, Suess, and Unzner (1985) discussed the German tradition for caregivers forcibly to encourage their children to become more independent toward the end of the first year of life. The increased proportion of avoidant infants in Grossmann et al.'s (1981) study is therefore likely to be a reflection of this practice rather than evidence for a generalised increase in the non-optimal attachment relationships in German infants. This is supported by the finding that German mothers who have grown up in a tradition where independence training is not emphasised are not at an increased risk of forming an avoidant attachment relationship with their children. Similarly, in traditional Japanese and Chinese families, infant and mother tend to experience continual bodily contact with one another throughout the first year; the infant is typically carried around in a sling and sleeps in the same room as the parents. Consequently, the events of the strange situation will be totally alien to infants brought up in this tradition, and, rather than providing a sensation of mild upset, the strange situation will cause them considerable distress. It is therefore hardly surprising that many more Japanese infants become extremely upset when separated from their mothers and cannot be comforted when they are reunited. This interpretation of Miyake et al.'s (1985) results is supported by a study conducted on Japanese women who had careers, which reported a distribution of attachment classifications comparable to American samples (Durrett, Otaki, & Richards, 1984). It therefore appears that differences in cultural child-rearing practices can account for increased proportions of insecurity within other countries, rather than any specific trait of German or Japanese characters. This is in line with the finding that the increase in insecure-resistant attachments in Chinese-American infants was related to the extent to which their families had retained their own cultural practices, rather than adopting prevailing American values.

Differences in parenting practices exist not only between cultures, but also within a particular culture. One of the major differences in child-rearing practices in Western countries centres on the mother's decision to work after the birth of her child. The effects of daycare on the security of the attachment relationship have received a great deal of attention (see Belsky, 1988; Clarke-Stewart, 1989, for reviews). The general consensus appears to be that high quality daycare has no adverse effects on the likelihood of a child forming a secure attachment relationship, provided daycare is not started too early in life. There is evidence, however, of an increased risk of insecure-avoidant attachment in children who are put into daycare before they are 12 months of age (Barglow, Vaughn, & Molitor, 1987; Belsky & Rovine, 1988; Vaughn, Gove, & Egeland, 1980).

It is extremely difficult to interpret the literature on daycare and attachment, since there are numerous extraneous variables which are likely to impact upon the security of the attachment relationship: the quality of care available to the child, the child's relationship with the carer in the daycare facility, the child's temperament, the mother's reasons for working, and so on. Unless all of these factors are controlled for, it is impossible to establish exactly how daycare *per se* affects the child's attachment behaviour. For example, no study in this area has included a measure of maternal reasons for working, but this seems to be of fundamental importance. A mother who decides to work because she feels that it will increase her self esteem and thus improve her relationship with her child should be considered separately from a mother who is forced to work because of financial hardship. Infant characteristics have also tended to be ignored in this body of research. For example, mothers may decide to send their children to nursery because they think their children's temperamental disposition will enable them to benefit from contact with other children. Again, this is very different from mothers who have to put their children into daycare when they are working and cannot afford to provide high quality care for their children. Clearly, all of these issues need to be ironed out in future research.

Perhaps the most useful conclusion that can be drawn from both the cross-cultural and daycare research is that it is unwise to assume that we can talk about *the* child and *the* mother as universal concepts. Many factors will affect both the child and mother as individuals, which will then impact upon the type of relationship they form with one another. Alternative explanations have thus focused on the effects of individual traits on the behaviours observed in the strange situation. The most well-known explanation of this kind comes from research on infant temperament.

Temperament

Infant temperament is of interest to those involved in attachment research because some temperamental characteristics may predispose an infant to establish a certain type of attachment relationship. For example, the temperament categories defined by Thomas and Chess (e.g. Thomas, Chess, Birch, Hertzig, & Korn, 1963; Thomas & Chess, 1977) place a child into one of three temperamental categories: easy, difficult and slow-to-warm-up. One could argue that the attachment relationship may appear to be secure simply because the child has an easy temperament. It is therefore important to account for the role played by temperament so that we can be confident that attachment behaviours really are indicative of the child's relationship to the caregiver.

Some authors have discussed the possible links between temperament and security of attachment, offering various interactionist accounts as well as "strong" temperament and "strong" attachment positions. Goldsmith and Campos (1982) discussed three alternative accounts for the observed differences between secure infant-mother dyads and their insecure counterparts. The first two accounts focused on the greater sensitivity characterising mothers whose children are securely attached (see pp.24 and 36–37). Goldsmith and Campos argued that: (1) the infant's temperament may directly affect a mother's sensitivity, which will in turn influence the attachment relationship; or (2) maternal sensitivity may affect infants' abilities to express both their temperament and attachment behaviour. Their third alternative gave temperament a more direct role: assessment procedures such as the strange situation utilise specific types of infant behaviour as the basis for an attachment classification, and are therefore measures of infant temperamental traits and not security of attachment. This "strong" temperament argument is based on the notion that behaviours observed in the strange situation involve infants' propensity to explore and interact, their emotional responses to separation from and reunion with the attachment figure, the speed with which they can be comforted, and so on. As such, these behaviours could be said to have much in common with the temperamental traits of adaptability, activity level and soothability (e.g. Thomas et al., 1963). Kagan (1982) has taken this "strong" temperament account even further, proposing that Ainsworth et al.'s (1978) attachment catgories are due to infants having different *innate* dispositions for reacting to separation.

It is in these cases, where the concepts of temperament and the infant-mother relationship are seen as mutually exclusive explanations for the types of behaviour observed in the strange situation, that the major problems arise. Sroufe (1985) argued that it was a mistake to try to reduce attachment behaviours to underlying temperament, since these systems function at different levels. Bowlby and Ainsworth both defined attachment as a *relationship*, whereas temperament is a feature of the *individual*. Moreover, Sroufe pointed out that both of these measures are important, and favoured an interactionist approach, since "viewing attachment classifications as reflections of the infant-caregiver relationship would not exclude viewing temperament as an important concept in explaining many aspects of infant or caregiver behavior" (1985, pp.2-3). It is worth noting that this view has obvious Vygotskian overtones, both in its emphasis on the dyadic relationship and in its recognition that individual biological characteristics affect the type of relationship that will be established.

Although this debate continues, it appears that the "strong" temperament position is untenable, owing to a number of findings. Firstly, temperamental distinctions of "easy" and "difficult" are not related to the security of the attachment relationship (Crockenberg, 1981; Vaughn, Lefever, Seifer, & Barglow, 1989). Secondly, life stresses have been found to affect the security of the attachment relationship with a particular caregiver (Vaughn, Egeland, Waters, & Sroufe, 1979). Thirdly, there is concordance between siblings' attachment classifications with their mother (Ward, 1983; Ward, Vaughn, & Robb, 1988). Finally, numerous studies have found that an infant may be securely attached to one parent, and insecurely attached to the other (e.g. Belsky & Rovine, 1987; Lamb, Hwang, Frodi, & Frodi, 1982; Main & Weston, 1982). Although some studies have found a concordance in infant security of attachment to both parents (e.g. Goosens & van IJzendoorn, 1990; Lamb, 1978), this consistency is generally agreed to be a result of similarities in parenting style between mother and father, rather than infant temperament (Fox, Kimmerly, & Schafer, 1991). All of these findings suggest that it is the dyadic relationship that is being measured in attachment assessment procedures, rather than simply the temperamental qualities of the infant.

The adult attachment interview

Just as infant characteristics may affect the attachment relationship, so too will certain aspects of the caregiver's psychological makeup. I have already discussed how maternal characteristics relating to sensitivity and responsiveness can affect the security of the attachment relationship, both with Ainsworth et al.'s (1978) original ABC range, and those characteristics linked to the type D classification. There is, however, another important caregiver characteristic that I have not yet touched upon, and which has received considerable attention in more recent years. According to Bowlby's "working models" theory (see pp.9–10), parents' early experiences of being cared for will affect their caregiving style with their own children. In order to test whether such intergenerational concordance exists, George, Kaplan, and Main (1985) developed the Adult Attachment Interview (AAI). The authors' intention in using this interview was not to assess adults' original attachment classifications in infancy, but to ascertain their present stance towards their own childhood experiences.

The AAI is a semi-structured interview in which adults are asked to recall various events from childhood, such as times when they felt rejected, what they used to do when they were upset, and so on. It is not the details of the events *per se* which are used as the basis for the AAI classification system, but the person's current emotional and psychological orientation to these events. Adults are placed into one of four categories: autonomous, dismissing, preoccupied and unresolved. The autonomous category is indicative of a well-balanced representation of attachment; adults in this category have not necessarily had ideal, loving childhoods, but they have come to terms with their early experiences and have no unresolved feelings. Indeed, some adults categorised as autonomous have had particularly difficult childhoods, and yet have managed to acquire the ability to deal with these experiences and move on. These adults are often described as "earned autonomous". The three remaining categories indicate that the adult has not fully come to terms with his or her early experiences. Consequently, they may: (1) dismiss the importance of intimate relationships by denying that they have any childhood memories or by idealising their attachment relationships; (2) become preoccupied and overwhelmed with issues relating to attachment relationships; or (3) have unresolved feelings which may relate to the death of someone who was close to them or to abuse they may have suffered. It is argued that the dismissing, autonomous and preoccupied categories of the AAI are related to the infant ABC categories respectively.

In support of Bowlby's notion of the intergenerational transfer of working models of attachment, concordance has been found between adults' classifications on the AAI and the security of the attachment relationship with their infants. In terms of a secure/insecure, autonomous/non-autonomous split, various studies have reported concordance between infants' security of attachment and their mothers' AAI classification, measured some time later (e.g. Main, Kaplan, & Cassidy, 1985; van IJzendoorn, Kranenburg, Zwart-Woudstra, van Busschbach, & Lambermon, 1991). There is even evidence that AAI classification is relatively independent of one's experiences of being a parent, thus supporting the notion that it is a measure of one's working model obtained in childhood. For example, two studies assessed primiparous mothers on the AAI during pregnancy and later assessed their infants' security of attachment. Levine, Tuber, Slade, and Ward (1991) reported an 83% concordance, and Fonagy, Steele, and Steele (1991) reported a 75% concordance between maternal AAI and infant attachment classifications. There is thus good evidence for intergenerational transfer of attachment relationships at the secure/insecure level, although the results relating to concordance between the separate insecure categories are more equivocal. Using a three-way split based on the ABC distinctions, Fonagy et al.'s concordance dropped to 66%, and van IJzendoorn et al. (1991) reported no significant correspondence between adult AAI and infant security of attachment when three categories were used.

While these levels of concordance in attachment patterns across generations are impressive and of considerable interest, adults' childhood experiences cannot entirely explain the security of their relationships with their children. For example, in the case of people who have "earned" their autonomous classification, we must ask what qualities enabled them to overcome early adversity. Similarly, since there is not a perfect concordance between adult AAI classification and infant security of attachment, what factors can account for those children who are secure despite their parents having a non-autonomous representation of their own attachment? Conversely, why do some children establish insecure attachments, in spite of their mothers' autonomous representation of their own attachment relationships?

HOW ARE THE ANTECEDENTS AND CONSEQUENCES OF SECURITY OF ATTACHMENT RELATED?

From the evidence discussed so far, it appears that there is no straightforward answer to the question: what makes a child securely attached? The security of the attachment relationship will depend on: (1) infant temperamental traits; (2) the caregiver's mental health, social support and childhood experiences; and (3) the type of relationship the two individuals can form, given their individual characteristics. Since infant temperament *per se* seems to have little effect on the security of the attachment relationship (see above), understanding why the caregiver's individual characteristics are related to security might tell us more about the processes which are fundamental to the establishment of a secure attachment relationship. This approach may also provide some insight into why certain indices are linked to secure children's subsequent development. Although the types of caregiver characteristics which have been found to be related to security of attachment are quite diverse, they do appear to have one thing in common: they will all affect the caregiver's level of sensitivity and responsiveness to the child. This conclusion would seem to make sense, since the role of early caregiver sensitivity in the later establishment of a secure attachment is one of the most enduring findings in the literature (e.g. Ainsworth et al., 1971; Isabella, 1993; Isabella & Belsky, 1991). But what is less clear is exactly why caregiver sensitivity is so important, or, more specifically, which aspects of sensitivity are crucial to this process.

Ainsworth, Bell, and Stayton (1974) defined maternal sensitivity as the ability to be aware of the infant's signals, interpret them accurately and respond to them in a prompt and appropriate manner. They asserted that the most important index of sensitivity was the mother's quality of interaction with her infant, and the appropriateness of her responses.

Thus, "the mother who responds inappropriately tries to socialise with the baby when he is hungry, play with him when he is tired, or feed him when he is trying to initiate social interaction" (Ainsworth et al., 1974, p.129). But clearly the caregiver's capacity to select an "appropriate" reaction is highly dependent on the particular infant and his or her ability or willingness to communicate accurately.

It is not immediately obvious why sensitivity should be so important in bringing about a secure attachment. It could also be argued that having a caregiver who interacts in a sensitive, responsive way will be important in telling the infant about the relationship between his or her actions and their corresponding reactions in the outside world. However, these interpretations do not have to be regarded as alternatives; rather, it seems likely that both are correct, simply because caregiver sensitivity covers such a broad spectrum of behaviours. For example, a caregiver may demonstrate her sensitivity by: (1) responding promptly to a cry that she recognises as signalling distress; (2) comforting the infant when upset; (3) making herself available for interaction; (4) interpreting the infant's actions as meaningful; or (5) treating the infant as an intentional agent. While all of these responses come under the umbrella of sensitivity, some are more clearly involved in the infant's emotional well-being, whereas others appear to be centred on the infant's cognitive life. It may be that sensitivity within the emotional realm can account for the establishment of a secure attachment relationship, and sensitivity in the cognitive realm results in the greater autonomy, independence and ego strength that are characteristic of securely attached infants as they develop (see pp.28–29). This brings me to a central point in my argument: that broad-based caregiver sensitivity may establish a secure infant-mother attachment, at the same time as helping infants to develop a sense of their own ability to bring about desired outcomes. In the chapters which follow, I will be referring to this latter understanding as the child's *self-efficacy*. Later I will discuss how a key determinant of this understanding might be the mother's ability to treat her child as a mental agent and attribute intentionality to his or her behaviour.

This discussion re-emphasises the importance of social processes in the development of cognition, which will be the major focus of interest in this book. The studies and discussions detailed in the following chapters can be seen to address two questions: first, do differences exist between securely and insecurely attached children in the realms of cognition and language? Second, if such security-based differences exist, how can they be explained?

CHAPTER THREE

Security of attachment and early cognitive development

> It is … very probable … that contact with persons plays an essential role in the processes of objectification and external-isation: the person constitutes the primary object … . It is to the extent that the object is externalised and becomes substantial that causality is detached from the action and is crystallised into independent centres. Thereafter, it is probable that another person represents the first of these centres and contributes more than anything else to dissociating causality from the movements of the child himself and objectifying it in the external world. (Piaget, 1955, p.252)

Researchers have always recognised that the establishment of the attachment relationship cannot be considered in isolation from the child's cognitive development, despite the fact that attachment behaviour is primarily a social process. Ainsworth (1963) emphasised that attachment behaviour is an active response by the infant, and therefore requires the recruitment of various cognitive resources, such as means-end computation and planning. Indeed, the infant as an active player is something that Ainsworth stressed very recently: "In seeing these babies on numerous occasions as they interacted with their mothers within the home, I think the thing that struck me the most was how *active* babies are and how much it is *they* who take the initiative.

They are not passive little things to whom you do things; in fact, in many ways they are the initiators of what happens to them" (Ainsworth, 1995, p.5, original emphasis).

Bowlby (1969) noted the relevance of Piaget's (1955) theory of sensori-motor development to the processes set in motion by the activation of the child's attachment systems. Just as Bowlby argued that attachment involves a shift from stimulus-response behaviour to a goal-corrected system, Piaget proposed that solving cognitive problems involves a transition from strategies based on trial and error, to those governed by insight into how means and ends are related. Bowlby also recognised that attachment behaviour was dependent upon the child having sufficient cognitive abilities to be able to represent an absent person. It is therefore reasonable to suspect that there will be parallels between attachment behaviour and the infant's search for objects, since both depend upon the ability to maintain contact with a desired object which cannot be seen. As well as providing a measure of the infant's capacity to form a mental representation of a hidden object, search provides an index of the child's ability to use this information in achieving a desired outcome. Similar skills are required by the child in the strange situation procedure. Here, as well as in the standard object search paradigm, it is necessary not only to have a representation of a goal to be attained (regaining contact with mother), but to be able to exercise one's established abilities in pursuit of that goal (e.g. approaching and following the mother, clinging to her once contact has been re-established).

PIAGET'S THEORY OF
SENSORI-MOTOR DEVELOPMENT

Piaget's four-stage theory of cognitive development has been well documented (e.g. Flavell, 1985). My own discussion of his work will be limited to the first stage described in his theory, the sensori-motor stage, reflecting my present concern with the relationship between cognitive development and security of attachment in *infancy*.

According to Piaget (1955), the major goal of the infant in the sensori-motor period is to come to understand the world of objects by acting upon them. In doing so, infants learn that objects have pre-existing properties that are independent of their actions on them. Piaget construed action as any intentional change in the perceptual input, placing it at the heart of his explanation of how infants come to understand objects (see Russell, 1996 for a recent discussion of this aspect of Piaget's theory). The most important achievement of the sensori-motor period is the attainment of the object concept: the understanding that objects are permanent and, unless they are moved, will remain in the location where they were last seen. Piaget saw this ability as central to the infant's capacity to think and learn, holding the object concept to be the "first invariant" of thinking. In order to have acquired the object concept, infants must regard objects as "permanent, substantial, external to the self, and firm in existence even though they do not directly affect perception" (Piaget, 1955, p.5). The first step toward achieving this understanding is the formation of a mental representation or picture of an absent object; the second is the process whereby the picture, in order to become an object, is "dissociated from the action itself and put in a context of spatial and causal relations independent of the immediate activity" (ibid., p.6). With this emphasis on action in general, and search in particular, Piaget investigated infants' knowledge of the physical world by observing how they searched for objects under different hiding conditions. The classic Piagetian search tasks involve hiding an object under a cloth or beneath an up-turned cup, and are based on object-hiding games which Piaget played with his own children. His observations led him to propose that infants have to pass through six sub-stages before they fully understand the affordances of objects, an achievement which marks the end of the sensori-motor period.

During the first sub-stage of the sensori-motor period (birth to approximately 2 months), infants are initially adualistic, but begin to draw a distinction between the self and the environment by interacting with the world using basic innate reflexive schemata, such as sucking and grasping. Piaget proposed that these basic schemata *assimilate* new objects, which in turn requires the original schema to *accommodate* to this new use. For example, the sucking schema will at first only be used in order to feed, but it will assimilate new objects (such as the infant's thumb or dummy), and this schema will in turn accommodate the properties of these new objects, leading to the establishment of mouthing as a way of learning about the world. These very limited modes of interaction with the environment ensure that infants of up to two months will not search for objects, although they may visually track a moving object.

During the second sub-stage (2 to 4 months), infants are equally incapable of searching for a hidden object, although they now begin to establish "self-world dualism" through an increasingly involved exploration of their bodies and the surroundings. The reflexes become more integrated *primary circular reactions*, which enable infants to have greater control over their environment. For example, they become able to combine the reflex of grasping an object with the action of moving the object to the mouth, so that it can be explored orally. However, objects only appear to exist for the child to the extent that they are involved in habitual activities such as mouthing.

The beginning of object search and infant thought are seen in sub-stage three of the sensori-motor period (4 to 8 months). Now infants come to realise that their actions cause events in the world—if they kick their cot, the mobile above them will move. Consequently, they begin to repeat their original movements for "action replays" of events which they found interesting and enjoyable. During this stage, infants also become able to retrieve *partially* occluded objects. Nevertheless, Piaget (1955) argued that their grasp of the properties of objects remains rudimentary, since "the child's universe is still only a totality of pictures emerging from nothingness at the moment of the action, to return to nothingness when the action is finished" (p.43). For an infant at this stage, out of sight is still out of mind.

Infants clear the major hurdle of object permanence in the fourth sub-stage (8 to 12 months), when they first become able to search for a *fully* occluded object. Piaget maintained that this becomes possible because the infant has mastered means-end behaviour. The child is therefore able to coordinate two actions to realise a goal: first the occluder must be removed, and then the object can be retrieved. However, whilst being capable of retrieving a hidden object when only one location is available, if they are given the choice of searching at one of two locations, infants of this age make a classic error: the stage IV or "A not B" error. In this task, an object is hidden at position A and retrieved by the infant for several trials; *in full view of the infant*, the object is then hidden at position B. On searching for the object, the infant persists in searching at position A. Piaget explained this error in terms of infants acting as if the object existed only as the outcome of previous successful searches, rather than as an entity existing independently of their own action.

Infants pass the "A not B" task during sub-stage five (12 -18 months), but in this penultimate stage of the object concept, Piaget argued that infants will only search for objects successfully if they have been able to *see* the object throughout the whole of the hiding procedure. If, for example, an object is hidden under cup B, and the position of this cup is then transposed with that of cup A, children of this age will fail to look under cup B in its *new* location. They do not appear to realise that the *invisible* displacement of an object is possible. In the final stage (18 -24 months), infants pass all of Piaget's permanence tasks, and understand that objects exist independently of their own action. Table 3.1 summarises the six sub-stages of Piaget's sensori-motor stage of development.

TABLE 3.1
A summary of the sub-stages of Piaget's (1955) sensori-motor stage

Sub-stage	Approximate age	Associated behaviour
I	0–2 months	Infants are adualistic, but can interact with the environment using innate reflexive schemata, e.g. sucking
II	2–4 months	Infants establish self-world dualism, and can perform primary circular reactions which combine the innate schemata
III	4–8 months	Infants recognise the relationship between their actions and events in the world, and can retrieve partially occluded objects
IV	8–12 months	Infants have mastered means-end behaviour, and can retrieve fully occluded objects. However, they fail the "A not B" search task
V	12–18 months	Infants become able to reach solutions to problems by trial and error, and pass the "A not B" task. However, they fail invisible displacement tasks
VI	18–24 months	Infants have insight into the consequences of actions without having to perform them. They can pass invisible displacement tasks, and recognise that an object's identity is independent of one's actions upon it

In addition to achieving object permanence, Piaget (1955) stated that infants would acquire the equally important concept of person permanence, or an understanding of the physical permanence of the "primary object". Indeed, Piaget suggested that person permanence is acquired at a faster rate than object permanence, because people are responsible for the child's emotional and physical well-being, and are therefore more salient than inanimate objects. This mismatch in developmental rate is an example of the phenomenon of "horizontal décalage" (Piaget, 1955). This means that, at a given age, children will achieve a higher level of performance on tasks which involve searching for people, than those which require them to retrieve a hidden object. Although Piaget himself did not study the development of person permanence, the findings of early studies in this area (e.g. Brossard, 1974; Goulet, 1974; Paradise & Curcio, 1974) seemed to lend support to his proposal of horizontal décalage.

Central to Piaget's theory of sensori-motor development, then, is the primacy of action in the acquisition of knowledge. That is, if a child cannot use a mental representation of an object to generate a physical action toward it, the child does not really "know" the object. This view of the conditions necessary for objective knowledge will be of particular relevance when I come to discuss the relationship between search and security of attachment later in this chapter.

RECENT EVALUATIONS OF PIAGET'S THEORY OF SENSORI-MOTOR DEVELOPMENT

Piaget's findings on the developmental progression of search behaviour are well-established. The controversy begins when one tries to explain why infants are unable to search for hidden objects until they are at least eight months of age. To recap, Piaget argued that, in order for the infant to be said to have knowledge of an object, he or she must be able to use what is known about its whereabouts to initiate search. Some, however, have argued that this reliance on action has resulted in a considerable underestimation of the infant's representational abilities. For example, Baillargeon (e.g. 1987, 1994) has suggested that infants have knowledge of object permanence quite early in life, but do not express this knowledge in action until much later.

Early knowledge of objects
In a number of experiments using the dishabituation technique, Baillargeon has demonstrated that very young infants appear to realise that objects continue to exist even when they can no longer be seen. In one experiment (Baillargeon, 1987), she demonstrated that infants as young as 14 to 18 weeks of age appear to realise that two objects cannot exist in the same place at the same time. Infants were habituated to a drawbridge swinging back and forth through 180 degrees, after which a block was placed behind the drawbridge. The amount of dishabituation shown by the infants was tested for a possible event (where the drawbridge was stopped by the block) or an impossible event (which showed the drawbridge seemingly passing through the block). The infants showed significantly higher levels of dishabituation to the impossible event, even though it was phenomenally identical to the drawbridge motion that had previously caused habituation (since the drawbridge swung through the full 180 degrees in both of these events). From these results, Baillargeon argued that even 14 week old infants have already grasped the object concept to some extent, since they appear to believe that two objects cannot exist in the same place at the same time.

There is evidence that young infants may even know what actions will be successful in retrieving hidden objects. Baillargeon, Graber, Devos, and Black (1990) found that 5½ month old infants dishabituated significantly more to an impossible object retrieval than to a possible one. During the familiarisation events, the infants were shown a single object which was then occluded by a screen, after which a hand passed behind the screen and re-emerged holding the object. In the impossible events, the object was first placed beneath a beaker or beyond an obstacle, and yet the hand re-emerged with the toy in the same way as before. The infants seemed particularly "surprised" at these impossible retrievals, since they looked at these events for considerably longer.

These results have been used to argue that, at the very least, Piaget underestimated the infant's ability to form a cognitive representation of an object in its absence, and that his theory should be questioned in light of these findings. However, this may not be the most fruitful conclusion to draw from this research. It may well be that Piaget's emphasis on search behaviour underestimated the representational abilities of the infant, but to disregard search behaviour as a valid index of ability does appear to be throwing the baby out with the bathwater. My own interest in Piaget's use of search as an index of development in the first years of life can be summarised as two questions: (1) does search tell us anything about infants' understanding of their own ability to achieve desired goals? and (2) does search behaviour have any connection to attachment behaviour? With respect to the first of these questions, if infants do have the ability to form mental representations from an early age, coupled with a good understanding of how objects can be retrieved, these facts only serve to make their failure to undertake any search action all the more interesting. In other words, it may be that the ability to search is dependent upon more than the comprehension that the object is hidden in a specific location, and acquisition of the necessary physical dexterity to remove the occluder. I suggest that the missing factor may be what I defined at the end of the previous chapter as *self-efficacy*, or infants' understanding of their own ability to achieve desired outcomes. If this is the case, we may be justified in taking search behaviour to be a valid index of these qualities.

The "A not B" error

Piaget's explanations of the later stages of the attainment of the object concept are no less controversial. As discussed above, Piaget explained the stage IV or "A not B" error in terms of infants' previously successful search actions, and their inability to divorce object locations from their actions upon them. In recent years, however, this explanation has been challenged by a number of researchers.

An obvious explanation for the infant's search errors is that he or she has simply forgotten the object's new hiding place. This is supported by the well-established finding that forcing infants to delay their search worsens their performance (e.g. Diamond, 1988). For example, an infant who passes the "A not B" task with a two second search delay may fail it if forced to wait five or ten seconds before searching. Explanations based on the infant's poor memory for the object's location find no support in Piaget's theory, which holds that the infant simply does not register the new location, and so this information is not able to interfere retroactively with the infant's choice of location on B trials.

The memory hypothesis has been tested in a number of ways. Cummings and Bjork (1983) provided infants with more than one incorrect location where they could search. They hypothesised that, if memory failure is the true cause of the stage IV error, then the infant's errors should betray some partial retention of the new location, resulting in the search errors being grouped around the correct location. The results supported their hypothesis and were taken to show that an artefact of the usual two choice hiding task was responsible for the A not B error. Such a conclusion does, however, seem to go against the findings of earlier experiments on the memory hypothesis. Butterworth (1977) and Harris (1974) had both previously found that infants will return to location A on a stage IV task even if *transparent* occluders are used. If this is the case, then surely the stage IV error cannot be explained in terms of a malfunction in some part of the infant's memory, since the infant continues to search at A even though the object can clearly be seen at B.

Diamond (1991) approached this issue from a different perspective. She investigated the possibility that the imperfect responses of infants on the "A not B" task may be due to immaturity of the frontal cortex, since this error mirrors perseveration found on certain tasks in adults with frontal lobe damage. Diamond suggested two alternative explanations of the stage IV error: failure is (1) a result of the infant's inability to relate and/or integrate information over space and time; or (2) due to the infant's inability to inhibit predominant action tendencies. With respect to this second proposal, Diamond noted that subjects must inhibit their habitual action to reach to A in this task, which can explain why infants still fail even when the object is visible at B (Butterworth, 1977; Harris, 1974). She drew an analogy between this type of error and the behaviour of frontal patients in the Wisconsin card sorting task (e.g. Milner, 1964). In this task, the subject is asked to sort a series of cards according to a rule, which is not explicitly stated by the experimenter. The cards can be sorted along any one of three dimensions: colour, form or number of elements, and the subject must establish the sorting rule by trial and error in the early stages of the task. The only guidance subjects are given is in being told whether the choice is correct or incorrect. However, once the subject has worked out this sorting rule, it suddenly changes, without warning. For example, the subject must inhibit the first rule of sorting the cards according to colour, and now sort them according to form. Typically, frontal patients will show a perseverative response to this sudden change to the sorting rule. Diamond argued that, both in the case of frontal patients and children who make the stage IV error, the initial action is reinforced, and so will always be stronger than the succeeding ability to resist a predominant response.

According to Diamond's view, it is not so much problems with the control of action *per se* that are responsible for the characteristic stage IV error, but the ability to relate vision and action and to inhibit the initial, predominant response. However, although Diamond's hypothesis is plausible, it is debatable whether the actions of infants and frontal patients can be compared in this way. It may be that, in such young infants, the schemata responsible for acting and choosing not to act are insufficiently distinguished. The same cannot be argued for the errors of adult frontal patients. That said, there are distinct similarities between the views of Diamond and those of Piaget, who regarded the object concept itself as the result of relating action and perceptual input. Both theories pinpoint successful "executive control" as the major determinant of object retrieval in the stage IV task. Diamond's theory holds that the infant possesses the relevant knowledge, but lacks the necessary executive control to succeed on the task, whereas Piaget argued that it is meaningless to speak of "knowledge" in the absence of such executive processes.

Factors affecting search

Given my specific interest in the relationship between search behaviour and security of attachment, the quest to explain the errors on Piaget's classic tasks lies beyond the scope of this book. Instead, we can ask whether any *individual differences* found on such tasks may be explained with reference to security of attachment. Diamond's work is particularly appealing in this respect, since her theory can account for any such individual differences in terms of how much behavioural control the infant is able to exercise. In other words, search behaviour may be viewed as a measure of the infant's ability to execute a plan of action to achieve a desired goal. Search for an occluded object will thus depend on three main factors: whether the infant (a) can mentally represent the currently invisible object; (b) is able to perform the requisite means-end act (over-riding prepotent responses); and (c) is inclined to recruit capacities (a) and (b) to regain sight of the object[1]. Ability (c) can be construed as a measure of self-efficacy, which was suggested in Chapter Two to be an important characteristic of securely attached children. If search behaviour is to be viewed as an index of self-efficacy rather than representational or executive abilities, we can turn our attention to my second question: what is the evidence for a link between search behaviour and security of attachment?

SEARCH BEHAVIOUR AND SECURITY OF ATTACHMENT

Intuitively, one would imagine that attachment behaviour must in some way be dependent upon the infant's ability to represent something in its absence. The child searches for a hidden object; the child cries for an absent mother. As noted earlier, Piaget's (1955) suggestion was that person permanence would be acquired before object permanence (the phenomenon of "horizontal décalage"), and this was supported by later research (e.g. Brossard, 1974).

One way of looking at this question is in terms of how *motivated* a child is to regain sight of the object. For example, one might predict that securely attached children would be quite willing to search if the target "object" were the child's mother. In contrast, given the tendency for insecure-avoidant children to avoid, and for insecure-resistant children to resist contact with their mothers, the mothers of these children would be arguably less likely to generate search. Bell (1970) tested a sample of 8- to 11-month-olds, and found that only the securely attached children attained higher levels of permanence when searching for their mothers than when searching for an object. The search behaviour of the insecurely attached children showed the converse décalage (object > person). The results of this study therefore suggested that Piaget's horizontal décalage was not a universal phenomenon.

Bell's data have since been questioned on methodological grounds, primarily because task demands for the object and person permanence tasks were not equated. In Bell's study, the infant had to retrieve an object from beneath a felt pad, but "retrieving" the mother required the child to search behind a variety of large objects—doors, sofas, screens; in fact, any large object which completely obscured the mother from sight. Indeed, the choice of occluder was only limited by the mother's willingness to cooperate in hiding, resulting in a lack of uniformity across subjects in the mother-hiding condition. Moreover, for any given child, the motor responses required for success *at the same level* on the object versus person permanence tasks were by no means equivalent.

Jackson, Campos, and Fischer (1978) highlighted how such methodological inconsistency can seriously affect a study's findings. They showed that if the task demands for object and person search were equated then, subject-by-subject, *no* décalage occurred significantly more often than décalage. That said, Jackson et al. did not include security of attachment as a variable in their study. The results of a more recent study show that the attachment relationship may in fact affect the child's ability to search, even if task demands are equated across hiding conditions. Levitt, Antonucci, and Clark (1984), using the same procedure for hiding the mother, a stranger and an object, found no décalage in the search behaviour of the securely attached children in their sample, but replicated Bell's findings for their insecure group. Children with insecure attachments attained a higher level of search for an object than for a person. Findings relating security of attachment and object-person décalage are therefore somewhat equivocal, and perhaps the only sound outcome of this research is that search demands in object and person permanence tasks must be made equivalent if valid conclusions are to be drawn.

SEARCH, SECURITY, AND SELF-EFFICACY

The answers to my two original questions can now be brought together. First, I asked whether search behaviour could tell us anything about infants' sense of their own self-efficacy. Second, I asked whether any such differences might be related to security of attachment. In considering the first of these questions, I concluded that indices of cognitive ability such as object permanence can only be regarded as accurate measures of actual competence if one can be sure that other "performance" factors can be completely ruled out. If securely attached children are viewed as more confident in their own efficacy, and thus more able to utilise their available cognitive resources in achieving a desired goal, then the level of permanence which they attain on search tasks can be taken as an accurate index of their representational and executive abilities. However, the same cannot necessarily be said for their insecurely attached peers. It may be that these children have the necessary knowledge about where the object or person is hiding, but lack the confidence or motivation to search.

As mentioned above, there is also the possible confounding factor of differences in secure and insecure children's motivation to search for their mothers. If we only consider the security of the attachment relationship, one may predict that securely attached children will be more motivated to search for their mothers than for other people and objects. There is, however, no obvious prediction for the direction of décalage in insecure children—how will their desire to retrieve their mothers compare with their desire to retrieve another person or an object? Then again, if self-efficacy is the key determinant of whether or not an infant will search, it may be that securely attached infants will be more likely to search *irrespective* of the nature of the target. Of course, a more stringent test of this hypothesis—that securely attached children are more likely to search because of their greater self-efficacy—would be to employ a paradigm where the representational and executive task demands are matched across the secure and insecure attachment groups. Such a balance would, however, be difficult to achieve in practice. Furthermore, given the findings of Baillargeon and others, we can at least suppose that infants' representational capacity is present well before they begin to search for occluded objects. The results of a study by Gopnik and Meltzoff (1987) also give reason to suppose that performance on object permanence tasks is not overly dependent on means-end skill, since these factors were found to be only weakly correlated with one another.

The first study to be reported here was undertaken to establish whether securely attached children are more successful at searching for hidden objects and people than their insecurely attached peers. The present study equated task demands across search for people and objects, and included a condition in which the child had to search after an *invisible* displacement of the object (a Stage V task: Piaget, 1955), thus extending the scope of Levitt et al.'s investigation.

STUDY ONE

The subjects for Study One were 48 infants from the Cambridge area, who fell into two age cohorts: 11 month olds (N = 27; mean age 42 weeks; range 40-43 weeks) and 13 month olds (N = 21; mean age 53 weeks; range 52-54 weeks). Socio-economic status (SES) was assessed on the basis of the mother's educational level and her previous or present occupation, and the father's occupation (Mueller & Parcel, 1981). That is, a family was considered to be "status 1" if the father and mother had manual/unskilled jobs and the mother had left school at the minimum leaving age, or "status 2" if the mother and father were in professional or managerial positions and the mother had either gone on to further education or had qualified to do so. No problematic combinations arose in the sample. Eighteen of the children (10 secure and 8 insecure) were status 1; 30 children (20 secure and 10 insecure) were status 2. There was no relationship between security of attachment and SES for the children who took part in Study One (χ^2 [1, N = 48] = 0.21, n.s.).

The infants' security of attachment was assessed twice using the strange situation procedure at sessions six months apart. The first cohort of children were tested at 11 and 16 months, and the second cohort at 13 and 19 months. These sessions were conducted in the department's developmental laboratory and were video-taped. The primary coding was done by the author, who has formal training in the strange situation coding procedure (Ainsworth, Blehar, Waters, & Wall, 1978), and a quarter of the tapes were coded by a second trained rater. Cohen's Kappa (κ) for inter-rater agreement was 0.81, and the remaining disagreements were resolved by discussion. Thirty infants were classified as securely attached, 9 children were insecure-avoidant, 5 were insecure-resistant and 4 were insecure-disorganised. This distribution across the attachment categories is consistent with those obtained in previous Western samples (see p.30). Infants' security of attachment remained stable between the two assessment periods for 98% of the children, and no child changed from being securely to insecurely attached[2].

Infants' search ability was also assessed at each of these two sessions. The objects for which the infants had to search were: the mother, a female stranger and a soft toy (in which the child showed an interest). Following Levitt et al. (1984), it was decided that the stranger-hiding condition should be included to give a measure of person permanence which was independent of the relationship between infant and mother. This therefore controlled for the possibility that the comparatively lower levels of person permanence observed in insecurely attached infants (e.g. Bell, 1970) may be due to their unwillingness to search for their mothers. The equipment used for the search tasks consisted of two movable curtained boxes, each measuring 2.5 × 2.5 × 5.0 feet (see Fig. 3.1). These enabled the object and person hiding tasks to be presented to the children in the same way. For the person permanence tasks, the mother or stranger was required to sit on a stool placed inside the box, and the baby had to draw back the curtain to regain sight of her. Similarly, when testing for object permanence, a shelf was fixed inside the box at approximately the same height as the person's head and the toy was placed on it. Each infant was tested on:

(1)   retrieval of an occluded object;
(2)   the "A-not-B" hiding task;
(3)   an invisible displacement task, with transposition of the boxes.

The transposition in this final task ("invisible displacement") involved the boxes (containing the hidden object or person) being wheeled across the room. All testing was done in a single session for each infant, and the presentation of the three hiding conditions was counterbalanced across infants.

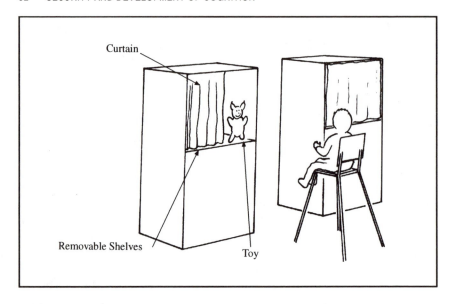

FIG. 3.1. The apparatus used in the object and person permanence tasks.

The object and person permanence tapes were scored according to the criteria outlined in Table 3.2 by two raters who were blind to the infants' attachment classifications. Each infant obtained a score of between 0 and 8 for the level of search achieved on each of the three permanence tasks. The child's highest search score was assessed, *regardless* of which condition (object, stranger or mother) it had been attained on. Each of these highest scores was then divided by 8 to convert it into a proportion of the maximum possible score: for example, if a child scored 6, the corresponding proportional highest search score would be 0.75.

The numbers of children in the three insecure attachment categories were too small for statistical analysis, and so a general "insecure" versus "secure" distinction was used. Although the main question was whether the securely attached children were more likely to search successfully, it was necessary first to determine whether the two groups were differentially influenced by the nature of the target. In order to establish whether there was any décalage between the mother and object or the stranger and object hiding conditions for the secure and insecure groups, chi square tests were performed. For the *mother-object décalage*: at phase 1 (11 or 13 months), χ^2 (1, N = 48) = 0.42 n.s.; at phase 2 (16 or 19 months), χ^2 (1, N = 48) = 0.23 n.s. For the *stranger-object décalage*: at phase 1, χ^2 (1, N = 48) = 0.60 n.s.; at phase 2, χ^2 (1, N = 48) = 2.39 n.s. Thus, it did not appear that securely attached children were more likely

TABLE 3.2
Scoring search

PHASE ONE (single occluder)	
Some relevant behaviour towards the curtain e.g. trying to peep round it, grasping but unable to organise its removal	1
Lifts curtain	2
PHASE TWO (A not B task)	
Searches at A, then B	3
Simultaneous search at A and B, not looking at B	4
Simultaneous search at A and B, looking at B	5
Search at B	6
PHASE THREE (transposition of occluders)	
Taking A as correct	
Simultaneous search at A and B, looking at A	7
Search at A	8

to search for their mothers, nor that insecurely attached children showed a preference for searching for targets other than their mothers.

For the comparison of general search ability between the two attachment groups, the measure of the child's search ability was taken as the *highest search score attained in the session, irrespective of the target.* The average proportional highest search scores were as follows: at 11 months, secure group 0.76, insecure group 0.58; at 13 months, secure group 0.80; insecure group 0.61; at 16 months, secure group 0.82, insecure group 0.78; and at 19 months, secure group 0.89, insecure group 0.61. A series of t-tests on these data showed that securely attached children attained significantly higher levels of search than their insecurely attached peers at all but one of the testing ages (16 months). The outcomes were as follows: at 11 months, $t[25] = 2.15, p < 0.05$; at 13 months, $t[19] = 2.15$, $p < 0.05$; at 16 months, $t[25] = 0.62$ (n.s.); at 19 months, $t[19] = 2.05$, $p < 0.05$. There were no significant differences between the two SES groups.

The main finding of this study was that children who were securely attached to their mothers were generally more likely to search for occluded objects and people than were children with insecure attachment relationships. Earlier in this chapter, I argued that search behaviour may be regarded as a measure of self-efficacy, in that it involves the infant not only having the requisite representational ability, but also the ability to *use* their knowledge to succeed on the task. The results of Study One are therefore consistent with the hypothesis that, compared with their insecurely attached peers, securely attached children have greater self-efficacy, in the sense of being able to use available resources to achieve a desired goal. Since no décalage effects were found, this result could not be an artefact of higher search scores for the securely attached children on the mother-hiding condition, but rather suggests their general superiority on Piagetian search tasks.

As mentioned above, it is possible to imagine alternative explanations for securely attached children's superior search behaviour. For example, their superiority could be explained in terms of their being (a) more capable of mentally representing the target in its absence, or (b) more skilled at performing the required means-end sequence. Given the age of the subjects in Study One, and what is known about much younger infants' object representational abilities (see pp.44–45), the first explanation would seem unlikely to be correct. What, then, of the second option? It is certainly possible to explain these observed differences in terms of the means-end skills underlying search behaviour, despite Gopnik and Melzoff's (1987) finding that search and means-end skills were not highly correlated. In order to address possibility (b), it would be necessary to obtain some measure of means-end ability (including the tendency to inhibit prepotent responses of the kind that might cause failure in the "A not B" task) that was *independent* of any measure of self-efficacy. But, as noted above, it is not at all clear how one might obtain a "pure" measure of means-end skill, uncontaminated by differences in children's confidence and inclination to make use of whatever means-end skills have been acquired. We are therefore drawn to the conclusion that, compared to their insecurely attached peers, securely attached children have a greater sense of their own self-efficacy, manifested in their greater ability to recruit the relevant cognitive resources to achieve the desired goal.

Of course, a further possible explanation of the observed differences is simply that the securely attached children were more intellectually advanced. Although these children were not assessed on standardised ability scales in infancy, they were subsequently tested on two such scales in early childhood (see Study Five). No differences were found between the secure and insecure groups on either of these standardised scales, a finding which is in line with earlier studies (see van IJzendoorn, Dijkstra, & Bus, 1995). An explanation based on differences in self-efficacy between the two groups is consistent with the finding of security-based differences on many tasks which do not involve obvious intellectual demands (e.g. LaFreniere & Sroufe, 1985; Sroufe, Fox, &

Pancake, 1983). More importantly, the notion of self-efficacy, unlike general intelligence, has the advantage of being conceptually linked with one of the core characteristics of a secure attachment, namely autonomy (e.g. Sroufe et al., 1983).

NOTES

1. I am grateful to Jim Russell for his suggestions on this topic.
2. It should be noted that this measure of security of attachment taken in infancy is the major independent variable for all of the studies reported in this book. Although the numbers of children in the secure and insecure groups change between studies, this is simply a reflection of attrition in numbers over time, rather than any alteration in children's attachment classification.

CHAPTER FOUR

Is security of attachment related to the infant's style of language acquisition?

> The initial function of speech is the communicative function. Speech is first and foremost a means of social interaction, a means of pronouncement and understanding ... Speech, as it were, combines within itself both the function of social interaction and the function of thinking. (Vygotsky, 1934, p.11)

In the first chapter of this book, I argued that a theory of attachment based on differences in ego strength provides a more satisfactory explanation of the infant-mother attachment relationship than the traditional "separation as trauma" model. The correlates and consequences of security of attachment were outlined in Chapter Two, with particular emphasis on securely attached children's greater autonomy and independence. I also discussed the possibility that the greater sensitivity of securely attached children's mothers may engender in these children a greater sense of self-efficacy in their interactions with the world (see p.37). The study reported in Chapter Three, which demonstrated the superior performance of securely attached children on Piagetian permanence tasks, lent some support to this characterisation. However, the limitation of using search as a measure of self-efficacy is that, in such tasks, one cannot assume that any individual differences may not better be accounted for by differences in other cognitive competencies, such as means-end ability.

In order to evaluate the suggestion that these differences in search behaviour reflect the greater self-efficacy of the secure group, we need to look for evidence of their superior performance in other areas where autonomy and self-efficacy can be exercised. An obvious way in which infants can exercise control over the people and objects in their environment is through their use of language. My aim in this chapter is to ask whether we might find instructive differences between securely and insecurely attached children in their early use of language, and how any such differences might be related to the security of the attachment relationship.

LINKS BETWEEN LINGUISTIC AND COGNITIVE DEVELOPMENT

The contention that there are cognitive prerequisites for language acquisition is a touchstone of Piaget's theory. It could be argued that this is the main reason why Piaget did not consider the role of language or communication in the child's development during the sensori-motor period: he believed that it was only possible to acquire something as complex as language if the basic cognitive structures were already in place. One such basic structure was the object concept (stage VI), which led researchers in the mid-1970s to investigate whether early knowledge about the permanence of objects was related to the infant's ability to refer to them. The end of the sensori-motor period certainly coincides with a dramatic increase in children's vocabulary size (the "naming explosion") and their ability to combine words (e.g. Goldfield & Reznick, 1990). But although many researchers have investigated the possibility that early language and cognition are related, an inherent difficulty in establishing causal connections has meant that the most enlightening studies on the relationship between the linguistic and cognitive domains are those which have investigated specific, rather than general, facets of cognition and early language.

Gopnik (1988), for example, has shown that there is a strong tendency for infants to start using a word for disappearance (usually "gone") at the same time that they begin to understand object permanence (stages III and IV). She argued that this indicates children's desires to express verbally their "theories" about how things happen. Gopnik and Meltzoff (1985, 1986, 1987) looked at the relationship between the onset of the naming explosion (typically around 18 months) and children's performance on object permanence and means-end tasks, such as using a stick to obtain an object. They found strong links between the onset of the naming explosion and performance on object permanence tasks, but no correlation between the naming explosion and means-end abilities. These results were taken to indicate that acquiring a *specific* linguistic term enables the child to move onto a higher cognitive level. Gopnik and Meltzoff suggested that the meaning of early relational words develops through three stages before the naming explosion occurs. At first these words are used socially, then they are used to encode plans, and finally the child uses them to talk about relationships between objects.

These findings throw up several discrepancies with the standard Piagetian account of the relationship between cognitive development and language acquisition. Firstly, it appears that children use early words to encode *developing* concepts, not those they have already established; secondly, words are used productively before stage VI cognitive ability is expressed elsewhere; lastly, the evidence is indicative of separate, dissociative relationships rather than a general relationship between stage VI cognition and language. In summarising their findings, Gopnik and Meltzoff (1985) concluded that "[i]nfants use their knowledge of the world to help them understand language but they also use their knowledge of language to help them understand the world" (p.220).

The connections between the domains of cognition and language may therefore be enriched by concentrating on the social aspects of language acquisition. It may be that the routes children take into language can give us some clue as to the role played by child-mother interaction in the acquisition process. It is to such a possibility that I now turn.

REFERENTIAL AND EXPRESSIVE STYLE

It is widely recognised that there is a balance between language as a regulator of social activity and language as a mode of representing objects and situations. Nelson (1973) was the first to document variations in the composition of different children's vocabularies during the one word phase. She argued that one of two pathways can be taken into language. After analysing the first 50 words acquired by the children in her study, she distinguished between *referential style* and *expressive style* (see Table 4.1). For these two linguistic groups, language appeared to serve different functions: referential children seemed intent on the process of object labelling, whilst expressive children's use of language was more directly concerned with social interaction.

Nelson found a number of other differences between these two groups. Referential style was correlated with first born status, parental educational level and rate of development, with referential children acquiring words more quickly than their expressive peers. Expressive

TABLE 4.1
Summary of individual differences in language development

Referential	Expressive
1. High proportion of nouns in first 50 words	Low proportion of nouns in first 50 words
2. Single words in early speech	Unanalysed phrases in early speech (e.g. "whatsat"; "heretis")
3. Imitation of object names	Unselective imitation
4. Meaningful elements only	Use of "dummy words" (meaningless words apparently used to increase length of utterance)
5. Rapid vocabulary growth	Slower vocabulary growth
6. Novel grammatical combinations	Frozen grammatical forms (e.g. "I love you"; "stop it")
7. Grammar learnt quickly	Grammar learnt more slowly
8. Object-oriented speech	Person-oriented speech
9. High intelligibility	Low intelligibility
10. Firstborn	Later-born
11. Higher SES	Lower SES

style was correlated with the incidence of imitative speech (although this finding has subsequently been questioned: Leonard, Schwartz, Folger, Newhoff, and Wilcox, 1979; Nelson, Baker, Denninger, Bonvillian, and Kaplan, 1985), and the speech of expressive children has been found to be more difficult to understand by people other than their caregivers (e.g. Horgan, 1979; Nelson, 1981; Peters, 1977). Bates, Bretherton, and Snyder (1988) argued that this lack of clarity is not because expressive children are "bad" at phonology, but because they emphasise different aspects of phonology (such as prosody or intonation) even at the one word phase.

Although the division between referential and expressive acquisitional style was operationalised in terms of the *continuous* value of the proportion of nominals to total vocabulary, Bates, Bretherton and Snyder (1988) pointed out that subsequent researchers have tended to treat this division as a *dichotomy*. Pine (1989) also recognised this potential misuse of Nelson's criteria, but criticised Nelson for perhaps over-simplifying the classification of words in the child's early vocabulary. His objection to the referential/expressive division was based on the fact that general nominals are likely to have been learnt in the context of specific labelling routines, and may thus give a false picture of referential children's general use of language. Pine argued that referential children may spend a relatively short amount of their time labelling objects, despite having a large vocabulary of object words. His other main criticism (Pine, 1992) was levelled at Nelson's assumption that the first 50 words can be regarded as being used unifunctionally. Pine pointed out that this is an over-simplification, because young children's use of words cannot be assumed to be context-independent. For example, depending on the situation, a child could use the word "door" as a label, as a commentary on the fact that someone has just left, or as a way of conveying a desire to go out.

Such criticisms resurfaced in Lieven, Pine, and Dresner Barnes' (1992) review, in which they concluded that, due to problems in accurately assigning items in the early vocabulary to specific linguistic categories, one should base the referential/expressive distinction on the presence of multi-word utterances. These multi-word utterances have become known as "frozen" phrases, and are characteristic of expressive acquisitional style. Frozen phrases include standard sayings such as "I love you" as well as more idiosyncratic word combinations (e.g. "Where's Mummy gone?"): what makes the latter fall into this category is the fact that these words do not occur *singly* in the child's vocabulary. Lieven et al.'s focus on multi-word utterances thus defines acquisitional style in terms of which words children pick up from the spoken language they hear, rather than how they themselves use the words they have acquired.

SECURITY OF ATTACHMENT AND LANGUAGE ACQUISITION

Very few studies have investigated the relationship between children's security of attachment and the way in which they acquire language. Van IJzendoorn, Dijkstra, and Bus' (1995) recent meta-analysis on this topic found only seven studies, two of which were unpublished and two of which investigated more sophisticated language skills beyond infancy. The results of these studies do not paint a consistent picture of the relationship between attachment and language, probably because of the diverse ways in which linguistic competence was measured. For example, Bretherton et al. (1979) found no difference between their secure and insecure groups in the number of words produced or comprehended at 11 months. They did, however, find that infants' use of declarative pointing at 11 months was the best predictor of a secure attachment relationship one month later. In contrast, Connell (1976) found that securely attached 18-month-olds had acquired a larger number of words than their insecurely attached peers. Gersten, Coster, Schneider-Rosen, Carlson, and Cicchetti (1986) reported that securely attached 2-year-olds had higher mean length utterance scores, but the aim of this study was to investigate the effect of low SES and early maltreatment on language development and attachment, suggesting that these results may not be generalisable to normative populations.

Of those studies concerned with language acquisition and attachment in infancy, only one unpublished study (Connell, 1976) considered whether securely and insecurely attached infants differed in acquisitional style along Nelson's (1973) referential-expressive dimension. Connell predicted that securely attached children would acquire language via the expressive route because of the superior quality of their interaction with their mothers. His results did not, however, support this prediction.

Research conducted since Connell's study has taught us a great deal more about the secure infant-mother attachment relationship and the characteristics of the securely attached child. This information makes the acquisitional style of securely attached children more difficult to predict. For example, if one focuses on the sensitive, responsive exchanges which are a defining feature of the secure relationship (e.g. Ainsworth, Bell, & Stayton, 1971, 1974), then one may expect, as Connell did, to see these children's interest in people reflected in an expressive acquisitional style. However, certain features of expressive style do not square with what we know about the securely attached child's character. Specifically, the imitation, lack of flexibility and poor level of comprehensibility in expressive speech seem at odds with the securely attached child's observed autonomy (e.g. Sroufe, Fox, & Pancake, 1983), ego strength (Lütkenhaus, Grossmann, & Grossmann, 1985) and self-efficacy.

In addition to this lack of congruence between expressive style and the established characteristics of the securely attached child, there are at least two reasons for predicting that securely attached children will acquire language via the *referential* rather than the expressive route. First, unlike their insecurely attached peers, securely attached children demonstrate secure base behaviour (see pp.22–23): the securely attached child tends to involve the mother in his or her explorations of the world by using her as a reference point. Secure base behaviour would thus appear to give the secure infant-mother dyad more opportunities to interact via objects, and provide the infant with an ideal arena in which to learn environment-related words. In contrast, insecure-resistant children typically show comparatively little interest in exploration, and will therefore not be presented with as many opportunities for learning words related to objects and events in the environment. Although insecure-avoidant children show considerable interest in the outside world, the fact that their explorations are not collaborative exploits involving the mother means that object- and event-labelling opportunities will be missed. Secure base behaviour may thus enable the securely attached child to acquire a greater proportion of object and event words, which have been shown to be characteristic of referential acquisitional style.

The second reason for predicting that securely attached children will acquire language referentially relates to their autonomy, ego-strength and self-efficacy, qualities which may make them more likely to take risks in acquiring language. Referential acquisitional style would appear to be the more risky route into language, since it does not rely on imitation and well-rehearsed phrases typical of expressive speech. In labelling an object in the environment, the child takes the risk of getting the label wrong in a way that an imitative child, or one who relies on frozen phrases, does not. Attachment-related characteristics may make securely attached children more willing to take such risks, since they are safe in the knowledge that their mothers will be there for encouragement and support.

The aim of Study Two was to address the question of whether individual differences in acquisitional style are systematically related to security of attachment. For the reasons outlined above, it is predicted that securely attached children will tend to acquire a high proportion of common nouns in their early vocabularies and not to rely on frozen phrases.

STUDY TWO

The linguistic acquisitional styles of the 48 children who took part in Study One were assessed. Thirty of the children were securely attached, eighteen were insecurely attached. With respect to SES, 18 children (10 secure and 8 insecure) were status 1 and 30 children (20 secure and 10 insecure) were status 2. There was no relationship between SES and security of attachment for the children who participated in Study Two.

The children's mothers were given a language questionnaire at the first testing phase (11 or 13 months) and were requested to monitor their children's use of language in the home by making a list of all the words and phrases their children used. The concept of frozen phrases was explained to each of the mothers: they were told that (1) children sometimes use certain words only in set combinations, and that children do not produce the individual words in isolation or in other word combinations; and (2) children may run a number of words together to produce a single "word", such as "whatsat", without using the items within this utterance individually. When it was clear that the mothers understood these definitions, they were asked to record whether their children acquired any such phrases. In addition, mothers were asked to make a general statement on how they perceived their children's language. A record of each child's language was made from the data collected by the mothers until the children reached 19 months of age. This record included the size and content of the child's vocabulary, the circumstances under which the words were used, and the first occurrence of a multi-word utterance. The children's total vocabularies at 19 months and the mothers' "general statements" were used in the analysis.

The majority of children in Study Two seemed to be slower at acquiring language than those who had taken part in Nelson's original study (Nelson, 1973). She used the first 50 words in the vocabulary in establishing her referential/expressive distinction, but most of the children in the study reported here fell short of this mark. The criterion was therefore taken as 25 words rather than 50. Three language scores were obtained, each giving some indication of "referential aspects" of linguistic style: (1) the speed of language acquisition (in terms of the number of words acquired by 19 months); (2) the proportion of common nouns in the first 25 words; and (3) the presence/absence of frozen phrases. Characteristics of a referential style were: fast language acquisition, a high proportion of common nouns and no frozen phrases in the first 25 words. Since this study used only three of Nelson's original measures of referentiality/expressivity (see Table 4.1), it was decided that it was inappropriate to divide the children into "referential" and "expressive" groups.

There was a wide variation in the number of words acquired by the children by 19 months of age. Children were classified as "faster" learners if they had exceeded the 25 word limit by 19 months of age, and "slower" if their vocabularies had not reached this point. Eight children had acquired only five or fewer words by this age and were classified as "late". In contrast to the "late" children, those children classed as "slower" language learners had acquired between 10 and 20 clear words, and were judged by their mothers to be very vocal and to have a tendency to imitate phrases and intonation. The "faster" language learners had 25 or more words in their vocabulary and tended not to imitate. The vocabularies of the "late" children were deemed to be too small to be scored for frozen phrases or for the proportion of common nouns, but the "faster" and "slower" language learners were divided into two groups according to whether they used frozen phrases. Any combinations of words which were used only in a set phrase (e.g. "stop it" or "Mummy, who's that?") were classified as frozen phrases.

Were there any differences between the secure and insecure groups in their linguistic acquisitional style? The results showed that securely attached children were more likely to manifest "referential aspects" of language acquisition. In terms of "faster" versus "slower" language acquisition, 77% of the secure group were "faster" language learners, whereas only 12% of the insecurely attached children fell into this category. For those children who were not classified as "late", a proportional score for the number of common nouns in their early vocabularies was obtained. The mean proportional score for common nouns was 0.63 for the secure group, and 0.31 for the insecure group. The vocabularies of all children except those in the "late" category were also scored for the presence of frozen phrases: 20% of the children in the secure group had acquired at least one frozen phrase, compared with 92% of the insecurely attached children. Statistical tests showed all three of these comparisons between the secure and insecure groups to be significant at the 0.005 level. There were no significant differences in acquisitional style between the two SES groups.

The final analysis centred on the mothers' statements about their children's use of language. Some mothers reported that their children were very vocal, but that they could only make out a few adult words and could not attribute a reliable meaning to many of the children's vocalisations. The propensity to report these "vocal but meaningless" utterances was found to be related to the security of the attachment relationship, with 63% of the insecure group mothers reporting "vocal but meaningless" utterances, compared with only 3% of the secure group mothers. This difference was significant at the 0.001 level.

It is worthwhile giving some indication of differences between children in the three insecure attachment groups, even though their numbers were too small for statistical analysis. Three of the nine insecure-avoidant children fell into the "late" category, and the remaining six children had all acquired at least one frozen phrase. The mean proportional score for common nouns for the insecure-avoidant children was 0.32, and 5 out of the 9 mothers reported "vocal but meaningless" utterances. For the insecure-resistant group, 1 child was "late" in acquisition, and the remaining 4 children all had at least one frozen phrase in their early vocabularies. Their mean common noun proportional score was 0.29, and all 5 of the mothers reported "vocal but meaningless" language. Finally, 2 of the insecure-disorganised children were "late", with the remaining 2 having acquired frozen phrases. Their mean common noun proportional score was 0.22, and one of the mothers reported "vocal but meaningless" utterances.

The principal findings of this study were that, compared with their insecurely attached peers: (1) securely attached children at 19 months of age tended to have larger vocabularies; (2) the vocabularies of securely attached children contained a relatively higher proportion of common nouns; (3) securely attached children tended not to have frozen phrases in their early vocabularies; and (4) mothers of securely attached children tended not to report the presence of "vocal but meaningless" utterances.

To analyse fully a child's acquisitional style, it would be necessary to chart their language acquisition well beyond the age of 19 months, and collect much more detailed data (see Table 4.1). Therefore, rather than attempting to draw simple conclusions about whether securely attached children are "referential" or "expressive" in acquisitional style, I will first discuss possible explanations for the four main findings of this study, before going on to consider possible commonalities between characterisations of the "referential child" and my earlier description of the securely attached child.

At first sight, the finding that securely attached children have larger vocabularies containing higher proportions of common nouns might be taken as a strong sign that such children acquire language referentially. However, even though Nelson (1973) identified fast language acquisition as a referential trait, it is clear that the larger the vocabulary a child has, the higher the likely proportion of nominals in that vocabulary (Pine, 1990). It is therefore possible that securely attached children's higher proportion of common nouns was simply a function of their fast language acquisition. Given the intractable nature of this problem, it may therefore be more helpful to follow Lieven et al.'s (1992) example and focus on multi-word utterances as the main index of acquisitional style.

When this route is taken, the observed differences between the two attachment groups appear to be more robust. Mothers of securely attached children were less likely to report frozen phrases in their children's speech. Before discussing possible explanations for this main finding, we should consider the related finding that such mothers were also less likely to report "vocal but meaningless" speech. Later I will argue that this difference may be less to do with children's actual speech than with their mothers' willingness to attribute communicative intent to their children's utterances. Mothers of securely attached children may be less likely to report such speech because they are more willing or able to recognise the intent behind the utterance and thus attribute meaning to it.

The results of this study provide some support for the prediction that securely attached children will take the referential route into language. Rather than trying to explain these findings directly in terms of security of attachment, my aim now is to sketch the main features of the referential child and the types of experiences he or she is likely to have, with a view to comparing this characterisation to what we have already seen of the securely attached child.

POSSIBLE CAUSES OF DIFFERENCES IN ACQUISITIONAL STYLE[1]

Numerous theories have been proposed to explain the differences in the routes taken by children in acquiring language. In her original monograph, Nelson suggested that maternal style may be responsible for such differences in language acquisition, since some mothers centre interactions with their children around objects whilst others use language in a more "interpersonal" way. Such differences in maternal style are clearly likely to affect whether the child takes the referential or expressive route into language. Furrow and Nelson (1984) investigated the differences between the language of mothers of children who typified expressive and referential styles, and discovered that although they did not differ in their own use of nouns, the two groups could be differentiated in terms of referential habits. Mothers in the referential group spent more time using language to refer to objects, and their counterparts in the expressive group made more references to people. The fact that mothers in these groups use language in different ways may affect their infants' developing understanding that language is a way of learning about the world as well as a mode of social exchange.

An everyday example of home life may clarify what can happen if the communicative intent of mothers' speech differs in this way. Imagine that Auntie Gladys has just left after visiting her sister and one-year-old niece, to whom she gave a yellow ball. The mother is now watching her child play with her new toy. The child who has acquired a good many terms relating to objects can use a number of different words to refer to this object—*ball, yellow, round, kick, sun*—all of which can be seen to be appropriate, and can be used to initiate an exchange with the mother. If the mother has a tendency to talk about objects, she will continue and extend this conversation about the ball. However, if she tends to use language to talk about people, she may choose to have a conversation about Auntie Gladys instead of the yellow ball. The child's mother could describe Auntie Gladys as a happy, ugly, married, female doctor, but what could the linguistically inexperienced child say about her? The child simply may not have acquired any words which can be used to describe Auntie Gladys, and will have to rely on "tested out" frozen phrases which may be inappropriate or inaccurate. The types of phrase which the expressive child is inclined to use are often quite endearing—"oh dear", "clever girl", "I love you"—and for that reason will tend to elicit a positive reaction in the listener. But in terms of learning about specific and generalisable attributes of objects, people and the world, these phrases give the child very little help. The mother will be the dominant party in this kind of exchange, and in this and future linguistic interactions, the child may take a largely passive role, since the notion that "language is for talking about people" will have been reinforced.

The fact that referential language tends to deal with the "here and now" may be an equally important factor in its usefulness in helping the child to learn about the world. In early language contexts, it is likely that the referent of a nominal will be present in the field of view. In contrast, conversations about people tend to occur when the person about whom one is talking is *not* present. To put it another way, one can talk about an object with impunity, but one has to be more careful about how one refers to people, especially in their presence. These points may give referential infants an added advantage in learning about the world, since the topics of conversation will be physically present, and there will be no social conventions determining what they are allowed to say.

This leads one to consider the role played by object-centred interaction in language acquisition. In the example I mentioned above, the shared context means that the child can have direct experience of how different words can be used to refer to the same object (the yellow ball). Werner and Kaplan (1963) referred to such contexts as the "primordial sharing situation", arguing that, by being exposed to situations in which different attributes are applied to the same object, the child takes the first step towards understanding that symbols can be used flexibly. Object-centred interaction is thus an important aspect of early development since it enables children to learn how to refer to environment-related phenomena, and teaches them the rudimentary facts about different perspectives on the world. Clearly, for this process to work most efficiently, the mother and child must be able to establish joint attention on objects and events, which will be related to the dyad's typical mode of social exchange and interaction.

Nelson (1973) suggested that, of the social interaction variables underlying the referential/expressive distinction, the most important was "active control" by the mother. She observed that mothers of expressive children were more likely to impose their topic of conversation on their children. Studies by Della Corte, Benedict, and Klein (1983) and Tomasello and Todd (1983) showed that mothers of referential children used more *descriptive* expressions to name, describe and comment on a given situation, whilst mothers of expressive children used more *prescriptive* expressions to direct or manipulate their child's attention or behaviour. In addition, Tomasello and Todd concluded that sustained bouts of joint attentional focus with an object are responsible for the child learning many early words, object words in particular.

To illustrate these points, if a mother and her referential child had focused their joint attention on a ball, then the mother's utterance would most likely be something like, "That's a ball" or simply, "Ball". In contrast, the mother of an expressive child may, for example, say, "Go and get the ball". The latter prescriptive statement is longer and also more complex than the former, and so the important term "ball" is not so easy for the child to pick up. Moreover, in the descriptive sentence, the word "ball" is much more likely to be stressed with rising intonation, as numerous studies of "motherese" have shown (e.g. Newport, 1976; Newport, Gleitman, & Gleitman, 1977). The stress pattern in the prescriptive statement is, however, not as clear, with the words "go", "get" and "ball" all being accentuated. Thus, even when the mother-expressive child dyad has achieved joint attention, the opportunity for the child to learn the object term may be missed. These studies suggest that, in determining the child's acquisitional style, the actual linguistic form of the mother's speech is less important than her use of language and her ability to share reference to an object with her child. It is not unreasonable to suggest that mothers who focus on their children's attention to the environment will provide them with terms to label objects.

Goldfield (1985, 1986) has reported some interesting evidence that sheds light on this issue. She (Goldfield, 1985) found that referential children were no more likely to engage in prolonged bouts of object play than expressive children, but they did tend to use toys to initiate social exchanges. She concluded that a referential vocabulary is not solely caused by a child being interested in objects or a mother providing object labels; instead it is a product of a dyad which uses objects as topics of "mutual interest, interaction and conversation" (p.30). Goldfield (1986) extended the context of the referential/expressive debate by looking not only at the content of the child's early lexicon, but also at child-mother interaction during video-taped play sessions in the home. Goldfield noted that children generally acquire a balance of referential and expressive items, and therefore chose to restrict her study to two children (selected to exemplify prototypical referential or expressive style). She concluded that mothers of expressive children may place secondary emphasis on naming, and that drawing attention to objects in a social context may be a predictor of referential language. Unlike their referential counterpart, the expressive dyad is therefore less inclined to use objects as topics of mutual interest or utilise them in a conversational framework.

These results point to a greater incidence of object-centred interaction being associated with referential acquisitional style. But it is difficult to explain why certain mothers might prefer to centre their interactions around objects, which in turn is related to the problem of establishing the *direction* of any causal link between infant-mother interaction and language acquisition. The child may first express a preference for using language to talk about objects, and the mother may then respond to this cue from the child; conversely, the mother's emphasis on object-oriented language may lead the child to focus on learning object terms. Furrow and Nelson (1984) recognised that such bidirectional effects are likely, and that a mother may nurture or enhance a particular style of language. But the mother's role in language acquisition may be important at an even more basic level, specifically because a mother's ability or willingness to collect accurate data can itself influence researchers' attempts to draw meaningful conclusions. In Study Two (as in the majority of studies in this area), the mothers were responsible for collecting the data on their children's language development. It is therefore impossible to control for differences in motivation and diligence between different mothers in monitoring their children's vocabularies. More importantly, it may be that some mothers are more willing to invest time and effort in trying to decipher their children's non-word vocalisations. Unfortunately, in a study of this nature there is no satisfactory way of controlling for problems which arise from the reliance on mothers for data collection; these methodological shortcomings must simply be borne in mind whilst one is interpreting the data.

These observed differences in mothers' propensity to interact via objects and imbue their infants vocalisations with meaning may impact upon other areas of infant-mother interaction. A key to such differences may be the message the mother seeks to convey: whether she uses language to prescribe what her child should and should not do, or instead restricts herself to a flow of language to describe the outside world and the events in it. Mothers of expressive children have been found to be more prescriptive (Nelson, 1973; Della Corte et al., 1983; Tomasello & Todd, 1983); their children may consequently experience less control over their environment, which may in turn affect their development of self-efficacy and ego strength. Although the findings relating to prescriptive/descriptive speech are well-established, again there are problems in establishing the direction of causation. For example, the mothers of expressive children may use prescriptive language because their children are less able to do things by themselves and need more direction. Conversely, in being overly prescriptive, these mothers may stifle their children's developing sense of self-efficacy. In contrast, mothers of referential children may confine their language to description because of their children's patent autonomy and confidence in performing tasks and achieving their own goals. Perhaps the direction of causation is somewhat easier to predict for referential dyads, given these children's propensity for using objects in social exchanges. Mothers of referential children may speak about object-centred events because referential children *themselves create* these situations by actively showing their mothers toys and initiating exchanges via objects (e.g. Goldfield, 1986). This contention leads us back to individual differences in the child which relate to self-efficacy.

Several factors may come into play in establishing the two-way interaction between the mother and child as an important context in which language acquisition can be facilitated. For example, if a child is beginning to use a label for an object, it is essential that he or she makes it clear what is being referred to, especially if the label does not correspond to the "adult" word for that particular object. This process may involve the child getting the mother's attention, achieving joint attention with her on the object, saying the particular word, and the mother making some response which recognises the child's intention to use that word to refer to that object. This lack of control experienced by expressive children will be compounded by the fact that their speech is more difficult to understand (e.g. Nelson, 1981; Peters, 1977). Expressive language will therefore be doubly limiting: not only will expressive children be less able to choose the topic of conversation than their referential peers, but they will be restricted in the number of people to whom they can talk. If it is only children's caregivers who can understand what they are saying, it is likely that they will not come to regard other people as sources of information or collaboration. This may result in these children becoming overly dependent on their caregivers, thus impeding their development of autonomy and self-efficacy.

The differential use of frozen phrases between the referential and expressive groups (Nelson, 1973; Pine, 1989) also provides a strong indication that differences in self-efficacy may exist between children who adopt these two routes into language. If children have a greater sense of themselves as effective agents, one would imagine they would want to do things for themselves and to initiate or take control of exchanges, at least for some of the time. The referential mode of language acquisition appears to enable children to achieve this, since a vocabulary containing a high proportion of common nouns allows for more flexible use of language and gives the child a means of describing and commenting on the world. Moreover, referential speech is the best way of learning more about the world, since it is more easily understood and will thus draw other people into linguistic exchanges.

In summary, the linguistically inexperienced child is not capable of using language for truly conversational purposes, other than by adopting *objects* as topics of conversation. Somewhat paradoxically, referential language may therefore allow for more effective communication than expressive language, in the sense that the child can initiate and direct interactions, even though he or she has acquired a relatively small number of words. A desire to take control of interactions and to express one's linguistic ability in the clearest possible manner may thus spur the child to acquire object names. The infant will then be able to choose an explicit topic of conversation, and since he or she has expressed an interest in talking about a specific thing, an adult may be more likely to continue and extend the exchange. Conversely, if a child exhibits expressive linguistic style, the lack of object terms (leading to a lack of conversational topics) and reliance on frozen phrases will constrain the use of language in initiating social exchanges. In showing a desire to take charge of linguistic exchanges, one could also argue that referential children are indicating greater self-efficacy, since they will be using their linguistic skills in a flexible and context-appropriate way, and optimising their chances of being understood. Of course, it is possible that this effect is bidirectional (Furrow & Nelson, 1984), but regardless of who establishes expressive or referential style as the acquisitional route, children who are exposed to an expressive linguistic environment will take a more passive role, resulting in lost opportunities to develop and exercise their autonomy.

ARE THERE COMMONALITIES BETWEEN THE REFERENTIAL CHILD AND THE SECURE CHILD?

From the preceding discussion, we can see that typical characteristics of referential children are their ability to use objects to initiate social exchanges, their willingness to take risks in language acquisition, and their ability to use language to develop and express their autonomy and self-efficacy. Referential children demonstrate the latter two uses of language in their flexible use of common nouns, their keenness to use these nominals to direct the topic of conversation, and their lack of imitative speech and well-rehearsed multi-word sayings. Coupled with this are a number of maternal characteristics which may be equally important in shaping the child's acquisitional style. Mothers of referential children tend to prefer to talk to their children about objects, using descriptive rather than prescriptive language. This description of the referential infant and mother tallies very well with my characterisation of the secure infant-mother dyad, and we already know from Study Two that securely attached children tend to acquire language "referentially". Autonomy is a well-known characteristic of securely attached children (e.g. Sroufe et al., 1983), and my argument for security-related differences being a reflection of securely attached children's self-efficacy (see pp.37 and 49–50) finds strong echoes in this picture of the referential child. For example, I argued that the insecure group's performance on the Piagetian permanence tasks used in Study One was likely to be an underestimate of their representational ability, and that search performance was not a pure measure of cognitive ability. Similarly, one could argue that performance factors come into play in the field of language acquisition, since a certain degree of risk is involved in naming a given object, and self-efficacy may therefore play a role in this process. Furthermore, the behaviour typical of the mothers of referential children is comparable with that of their counterparts with securely attached children. The central defining featue of securely attached children's mothers is their sensitivity and responsiveness to their children's desires and needs (e.g. Ainsworth, Bell, & Stayton, 1971). In Chapter Two, I argued that this sensitivity may be dependent upon the mother's propensity to treat her infant as a mental agent. The ways in which mothers of referential children act—describing the world, refraining from using language as a means of control, and so on—could also be taken as evidence for these mothers treating their children as mental agents. The fact that the results of Study Two showed mothers in the secure group to be more likely to attribute meaning to their children's utterances (tending not to report "verbal but meaningless" speech) suggests that the ability or willingness to treat one's child as a mental agent may affect both the attachment relationship and the route that the child takes into language. Viewing the results of Study Two as a further manifestation of the securely attached children's greater self-efficacy, and their mothers' willingness to treat them as intentional agents, may thus provide a plausible explanation of these security-related differences in acquisitional style. The results of Bretherton et al. (1979) on the relationship between declarative pointing and subsequent security of attachment are consistent with this explanation, since one would imagine that children will only come to be skilful users of declarative pointing if their previous uses of gesture have been interpreted as being intentional.

While infants are becoming interested in using language, people around them will be referring to the same object using a number of different words. Clearly, if the mother is able to recognise that her child is referring to given objects and then concentrates on using objects as "topics of conversation", not only will this lead the child to acquire object terms, but it will help him or her to understand that different things can be represented in different ways. The next step will be for the child to grasp the fact that others may adopt different mental orientations towards the same object or event.

NOTE

1. For the sake of simplicity, I shall continue to use the terms "referential" and "expressive" to define acquisitional style. Rather than implying a strict dichotomy, my use of these terms merely reflects the fact that referential children have acquired proportionally more object words in their early vocabularies and no frozen phrases, whereas expressive children's vocabularies tend to contain frozen phrases and fewer object words.

CHAPTER FIVE

Symbolic play and security: A meeting of minds?

> As in the focus of a magnifying glass, play contains all developmental tendencies in a condensed form; in play it is as though the child were trying to jump above the level of his normal behaviour. The play-development relationship can be compared to the instruction-development relationship, but play provides a background for changes in needs and in consciousness of a much wider nature. Play is the source of development and creates the zone of proximal development. (Vygotsky, 1933, p.552)

There have been numerous attempts to document relationships between the development of language and play. In their earliest dealings with objects, infants appear not to differentiate between one type of object and another (Uzgiris, 1976). These rudimentary forms of object play, such as mouthing and simple manipulation, will develop into functional play, where infants shape their actions to fit the object. Eventually, play actions are divorced from the object itself, and infants become able to pretend that one object is something entirely different, or to evoke a pretend object out of thin air. It is this more sophisticated type of pretend or *symbolic* play which has attracted the greatest amount of attention, with early studies in this area largely influenced by Piaget's (1962) views this topic. Researchers interested in the relationship between language and play have accordingly tended to focus on the occurrence of symbolic play, rather than the more rudimentary sensori-motor and functional forms of play.

Early types of symbolic play, such as "drinking" out of an empty toy cup and imitating gestures, are first seen at about the same time at which children acquire their first words. If a child's language development is delayed, similar lags are seen in symbolic play and imitation (Bates, O'Connell, & Shore, 1987; Snyder, 1978; Ungerer & Sigman, 1984). When children start to combine words at around 18 months of age, they also start to combine symbolic gestures into a sequence of pretend play, pouring "tea" from the teapot into a cup, and then "drinking" the "tea". Several researchers (Bates et al., 1987; Brownell, 1988; Shore, 1986) have found that those children who combine gestures in this way at relatively early ages are more likely to produce multi-word utterances precociously. There is thus some reason to suppose that the processes of language and play development depend upon similar underlying capacities, specifically those involved with symbolising abilities.

Several quite recent studies have investigated the relationship between early language skills and the onset of pretence. For example, Tamis-LeMonda and Bornstein (1990) demonstrated specific relationships between flexible language comprehension and symbolic play. These authors argued that early variability in language *production* is not necessarily related to any underlying representational ability; some children may simply bide their time before speaking so that they can be sure of getting it right (Bates, Thal, Fenson, Whitesell, & Oakes, 1989). It is for similar reasons that I cautioned against regarding insecurely attached children's search behaviour in Study One as an accurate index of their cognitive representational ability (see p.49), and suggested that such an explanation might account for the security-related differences in linguistic acquisitional style observed in Study Two. For example, children who are less willing to take chances in language acquisition may be more likely to use the expressive route; the frozen phrases which are typical of this route into language are "safer" because they are well-tested and do not need to be context-specific. Given that language and play are assumed to be mediated by similar types of symbolic functioning, can we expect security-related differences in play?

Many researchers have set about investigating how maternal modes of interaction affect their children's abilities in play. Bruner (1973) concentrated on the social contextual factors of play, maintaining that play and exploration provide a testing ground for the child to practise various behavioural routines involved in social interactions. The notion of play as an index of both social and cognitive development has been adopted by Belsky and colleagues. Belsky, Goode, and Most (1980) hypothesised that if a mother is able to focus her infant's attention on aspects of the physical world, by physical or verbal means, the amount of time the infant spends manipulating toys will increase and the quality of play will improve. They also predicted that, as the child becomes more linguistically aware, the mother will decrease the amount of physical stimulation she gives her child, with a corresponding increase in verbal stimulation. In support of the first hypothesis, their results showed that the infants who were most competent in exploration had mothers who frequently focused their attention on objects. Moreover, as the children started using language, their mothers began to interact using verbal devices exclusively, thus supporting their second prediction. Belsky et al.'s (1980) study thus provides a further reason for expecting security-based differences in play, since we know that a securely attached mother-infant pair tends to share reference with objects and exchange comments and vocalisations (Ainsworth et al., 1978). I have also suggested that it is important for the mother to confine herself to general guidance and support during these interactions, and limit her prescriptive comments, allowing the child space for self-expression and experimentation. In other words, the mother must gauge when to give her child free rein to play and explore without her instruction and intervention.

In Chapter Three, I discussed the possibility that securely attached children's superior performance on search tasks could also be explained with reference to differences in self-efficacy between the secure and insecure groups. It may therefore be possible to link all of these areas. For a child to be able to pretend, he or she must be able to represent an object in different ways, treating one object as if it were something else. Vygotsky (1933) noted how children must sever the meaning of an object from how it is normally perceived in order for it to be used in pretence. A variation of this view has been expressed more recently by Leslie (1987), who maintained that in order to be able to pretend, one must be able to form metarepresentations which are unconstrained by reality. Common to both of these views is the notion that the "pretend" object is one that is not present. Why should a child bother to pretend that there is liquid in a cup if real liquid is available? Why should children pretend that a broom is a horse if they have immediate access to a hobby horse? In essence, the ability to engage in symbolic play is dependent upon the ability to evoke objects in their absence.

Not only is symbolic play a measure of children's understanding that different perspectives on the world exist (since it involves being able to adopt different orientations to the same element of reality), but it may reflect their ability to use their knowledge about absent objects and people to inform their action sequences. Tamis-LeMonda and Bornstein

(1989) have also discussed the possibility that the representational capacities involved in both language and pretend play "may be subserved by the same underlying ability to abstract from the immediate context" (p.739). If these areas of development do indeed have common ancestors in infancy, given the results of Studies One and Two, one may predict that the security of the attachment relationship may affect certain aspects of the child's symbolic play.

Another reason to suggest that there may be differences in play between the secure and insecure groups is that symbolic play may reflect children's autonomy, a characteristic feature of securely attached children (e.g. Matas, Arend, & Sroufe, 1978). Thus, "[b]ecause symbolic play offers the child a means of playing and thinking about absent objects and people, and of representing self, it is one of the earliest tools of the child's autonomy" (Slade, 1987a, p.368). What form might such differences in autonomy take? Will securely attached children simply be more sophisticated in their use of pretence and symbolism in play, or will any differences between securely and insecurely attached children be more subtle?

FACTORS INFLUENCING SYMBOLIC PLAY

The major influences on the content and level of sophistication of a child's symbolic play can be divided into two broad areas: (1) environment-centred factors; and (2) child-centred factors. The factors which fall into the first category are very wide-ranging, and include the child's present and previous contact with objects and people. It would seem reasonable to assume that if children are not given stimulating toys which offer them opportunities for pretence, then this may impair their symbolic play. But since it seems obvious that the vast majority of children will have such objects available, any differences found in the sophistication of symbolic play must be due to other factors. Perhaps the most obvious of the environment-centred factors is the role played by the child's mother or caregiver.

Tamis-LeMonda and Bornstein (1989) investigated the effect of maternal encouragement of attention when children were 5 months of age on the child's language comprehension, language production and pretend play at 13 months. Although a significant association was found between a "representational competence" variable (consisting of language production and symbolic play measures) and maternal encouragement, there was no significant relationship when only the pretend play measure was used. This result is surprising, and led Tamis-LeMonda and Bornstein to conclude that, rather than the mother having no influence on her child's symbolic play, other types of maternal behaviour may be better predictors of symbolic play; specifically, these authors implicated behaviours involving maternal responsiveness to the child. Clearly, one would assume that such differences in responsiveness will reflect the security of the attachment relationship. Isabella (1993), for example, discussed how mothers of insecurely attached children are not ideally responsive to their children's needs: mothers of insecure-avoidant children tend to be unresponsive, whereas mothers of insecure-resistant children are inconsistent in their patterns of interaction. Children with such insecure attachments would therefore appear to have less exposure to consistently responsive mothering, which, according to Tamis-LeMonda and Bornstein, may hinder their symbolic play abilities.

In a later study, Tamis-LeMonda and Bornstein (1994) considered which types of maternal behaviours may be important in nurturing the child's symbolic capacities. They found that the absolute amount of maternal stimulation was a poor predictor of the child's symbolic play; instead the *nature* of the stimulation was the crucial factor, with the child's symbolic play being related to the mother's specific play prompts, and not to her tendency merely to talk about objects. Of greater interest is the finding that the mother's level of sophistication of modelling and encouraging symbolic play acts at 13 months showed an *inverse* relationship to toddler's productive vocabulary size at 20 months of age. Tamis-LeMonda and Bornstein explained this finding by suggesting that high levels of symbolic play by the mother may actually confuse the young child, whereas if a mother limits the content of play to object labelling at 13 months, then the child's subsequent symbolic play is more likely to benefit.

As the discussion in Chapter Four suggested, this type of object-centred maternal interaction would be expected in secure infant-mother attachment relationships. In addition, Tamis-LeMonda and Bornstein's study showed that mothers who limited their interaction at 13 months to object labelling changed strategy at 20 months to more direct encouragement of symbolic play. Tamis-LeMonda and Bornstein concluded that "children at 13 months, who are already advanced in language and play, may lead mother to later prompt and maintain pretense-based exchanges" (1994, p.288). This study shows how, in acquiring an understanding of symbolic representation, environment-centred factors and child-centred factors are intimately linked: the initial pace is set by the child's level of ability in language and play, whilst the mother adapts to the child's increasing skills and competence.

However, play can be seen as an index of the child's *motivation* as well as ability, and considering the motivation to play may give us clues as to how any differences between securely and insecurely attached children might be manifested in symbolic play. Two studies performed by Belsky and his colleagues are of relevance here. Belsky and Most (1981) attempted to establish a developmental progression of infant exploration and play, but concluded that the individual child's level of symbolic play was only modestly predicted by age, with several of the younger toddlers outstripping their older counterparts. They argued that these age-independent differences are particularly interesting, since, by using free play, one not only taps into the child's competence in the use of toys and social skills, but measures the child's motivation to engage in sequences of pretence. Subsequently, Belsky, Garduque, and Hrncir (1984) proposed that the difference between performance and competence can be seen as an index of the individual's motivation to function at an optimal level, and investigated whether differences between securely and insecurely attached children existed on this measure.

Belsky et al.'s study used a three-trial strategy to encourage infants between 12 and 18 months of age to engage in a specific play act using a selection of toys, the majority of which were miniatures of "adult" objects. Verbal encouragement was the first step (e.g. "the doll's thirsty, give the doll a drink"), followed by modelling of the desired act by the experimenter if there was no response to the verbal suggestion. If the child still failed to engage in the specific play act, then the two elicitation strategies were combined, i.e. verbal suggestion plus modelling. The authors showed that, in solo play, securely attached children produced a level of pretence near to that which could be evoked from them by adult intervention. In contrast, the solo play of insecurely attached children showed a much lower level of pretence than that of their assisted play. From these results, Belsky et al. concluded that securely attached children possess a smaller competence-performance gap, and appear to be more motivated spontaneously to function near their maximum level in a pretend play context.

Belsky et al. used the term *executive capacity* to define the difference between what the child was capable of ("competence", i.e. instructed play) and what the child routinely displayed ("performance", i.e. spontaneous play). They chose this term in order to reflect "the infant's capacity to execute, in a self-initiated manner, his or her most advanced level of functioning" (p.407). Their notion of executive does not therefore have any of the overtones usually associated with the use of this term in fields such as cognitive neuropsychology (e.g. Shallice, 1988).

AGE-RELATED CHANGES IN SYMBOLIC PLAY

On the basis of these results, it would appear that securely attached children are simply better at pretending in solo play than their insecurely attached peers. A question which leads on from this is whether this superior competence will persist as the child gets older, or whether securely attached children will out-perform their insecurely attached peers in different ways as they develop. A third option is that insecurely attached children may simply catch up with their securely attached peers, thus overcoming their early disadvantage. Evidence from Tamis-LeMonda and Bornstein (1994) gives us reason to suggest that the mode of expression of securely attached children's superiority in symbolic play will change over time. As mentioned above, these authors found that children showing higher levels of symbolic play at 13 months of age—like the securely attached children in Belsky et al.'s study—had mothers who were more likely to encourage symbolic play when the children reached 20 months of age. It may therefore be the case that the securely attached children's superiority in symbolic play at 12 to 18 months of age will be converted into a more subtle kind of advantage in pretence when they are older. Specifically, this advantage may stem from an ability to interact with others in sequences of symbolic play, for example, the child acting upon the mother's suggestion for a sequence of play.

The results of a study by Slade (1987b) address this suggestion. Slade performed a longitudinal study to investigate how security of attachment affected children's subsequent development of symbolic play between 20 and 28 months of age. Slade reported that there were no security-based differences in the frequency of symbolic play in these older children, but the securely attached children were more likely to organise their play around a theme, especially at older ages. These results suggest that, although insecurely attached children may catch up with their securely attached peers with respect to the overall frequency with which they engage in symbolic play, there are still security-based differences in the approach to pretence. Of perhaps greater interest are Slade's findings on the effect of maternal involvement on children's play in the secure and insecure groups. Once again, at the level of solo play, there were no security-based differences. However, maternal involvement facilitated the play of securely attached children more than that of children with insecure attachments. Slade concluded that the differences between the secure and insecure groups were related to "the ways cognitive competencies *interact with* social competencies" (ibid. p.83, original emphasis), and were independent of general cognitive ability.

Slade's study clearly showed the differential benefit of maternal involvement in securely and insecurely attached children's play, while acknowledging the need for further research to establish whether securely attached children's ability to benefit from maternal interaction generalised to other people. It may be that the ways in which securely attached children's mothers collaborate and interact with them in play contexts will enable these children to benefit from a similar input from other sources. Accordingly, the aim of Study Three was to establish whether any differences in symbolic play persist between securely and insecurely attached children when they are well into their third year of life, and to assess these children's ability to act upon an experimenter's play suggestions.

The play materials and method of encouraging symbolic play were adapted from a study by Lewis and Boucher (1988), who argued that, since previous studies exclusively used "real" toys and miniatures of real objects, the so-called "pretend" play which was observed may have been biased towards *functional* and not symbolic types of pretence. To establish whether the selection of toys had any effect on the way in which different children became involved in sequences of pretence and *symbolic* play, Lewis and Boucher used a set of "junk" objects in addition to conventional toys. Lewis and Boucher were also concerned that in previous studies the experimenter may have constrained children's levels of pretence by giving them instructions to follow and modelling the exact kind of response that was desired. The experimenter in their study therefore refrained from using any modelling and chose to elicit play in a more open-ended way, leaving the initial imaginative input to the child.

STUDY THREE[1]

The subjects were 43 (14 girls and 29 boys) of the original 48 infants who participated in Studies One and Two. The average age of the children was 2 years, 7 months (range: 2 years, 5 months to 2 years, 9 months). Of the 43 subjects, 27 were securely attached, 8 were insecure-avoidant, 5 were insecure-resistant and 3 were insecure-disorganised. With respect to SES (see p.50), 16 children (9 secure and 7 insecure) were status 1 and 27 (18 secure, 9 insecure) were status 2. There was no relationship between security of attachment and SES for the children who took part in Study Three.

The study was performed in the child's home. Mothers were present during the session and were allowed to give their children general encouragement and respond to their questions and comments, but were told not to give any specific suggestions as to what could be done with the objects. They were told that the study was concerned with children's levels of solo play and that the experimenter would be suggesting things for the child to do with the objects to see if he or she would benefit.

All of the toys were laid down, and the child was encouraged to come to look at what was on the floor. Children were told that they could play with anything they liked, and were allowed approximately five minutes of spontaneous play. The set of objects consisted of two representational toys (a toy car and a female doll) plus a strip of cardboard, small cardboard box, toilet roll inner tube, coffee jar lid, seven coloured building blocks, a plastic lunch box, piece of aluminium foil, blue napkin and a flattened-out paper bun case (see Table 5.1). The child's play was video-taped using a portable video camera, and the session began the moment one of the objects was first touched intentionally.

Structured play
The structured play session began immediately after the initial spontaneous play session. There were two types of structured play: *elicited* and *instructed*. In the former condition, the child was given no instructions as to how the materials could be used; in the latter, the child was expressly asked to perform a given act with the objects. For example, the child was given either the car + an object or the doll + an object and was asked "What can you do with these?" (elicited condition). When the child had performed some action with the objects in question, or if it became clear that any action would not or could not be performed, the experimenter asked the child to perform a specific act (see Table 5.1)—

TABLE 5.1
Questions for instructed pretend play

Selection of toys	Instructed question
Car + cardboard box	Make the car go in the garage
Car + cardboard strip	Make the car drive along the road
Car + coffee jar lid	Make the car go round the roundabout
Car + inner tube	Make the car go through the tunnel
Car + 7 bricks	Make a car park for the car to go in
Doll + lunch box	Make the doll have a bath
Doll + bun case	Make the doll eat her dinner off the plate
Doll + aluminium foil	Make the doll look at herself in the mirror
Doll + blue napkin	Make the doll go for a swim in the pool

this was the instructed condition. The order of presentation of the toy-object pairs was randomised.

Assessment of executive capacity

In the instructed condition, the scoring procedure was a measure of children's ability to use another person's suggestion within the context of pretend play, rather than of the capacity for pretend play *per se*. Table 5.2 gives two examples of the scoring protocol. For each toy-accessory pair, children could score a maximum of four if they succeeded in following the experimenter's suggestions precisely. In the present study, the executive capacity for each child was calculated by adding up the scores obtained in the elicited play sessions (the level of performance) and the scores obtained after the instructed play sessions (the level of competence), taking into account the potential number of stages through which the child could advance from the elicited play score. Thus,

$$\text{Executive capacity} = \frac{\text{Score instructed play—Score elicited play}}{\text{Number of levels remaining}}$$

The formula differs slightly from that used by Belsky et al. (1984), since the score for spontaneous play score was replaced with that for elicited play.

On the elicited play condition, the mean scores were: 8.04 for the secure group and 6.94 for the insecure group. The difference in means between the secure and insecure groups for *elicited* play was not significant. On the instructed play condition, the mean scores were:

TABLE 5.2
A sample of the scoring criteria for pretend play

Toy car		
Inner tube "tunnel"	0	Pushes car along floor
	1	Pushes car over the tube, or some other interaction between the two objects
	2	Tube held upright on floor, car dropped in
	3	Tube on floor on its side, car pushed along into it
	4	As 3, but "drives" car out
Toy doll		
Lunch box "bath"	0	Plays with doll
	1	Some interaction between doll and box
	2	Places box in correct orientation
	3	Places doll in box
	4	"Prepares" doll for bath and places her in box, or "splashing/washing" doll when in box

22.42 for the secure group and 12.76 for the insecure group. This difference in *instructed* play was significant at the 0.001 level. The securely attached children therefore benefited more from instruction than their insecurely attached peers. Finally, the mean executive capacity scores were 0.50 for the secure group, and 0.17 for the insecure group, which represented a difference at the 0.001 level of significance. None of these results could be explained in terms of differences in SES.

The mean scores for the three insecure attachment groups should also be mentioned. For the insecure-avoidant group (N = 8): the mean elicited play score was 5.80; the mean instructed play score was 11.80; and the mean executive capacity score was 0.18. For the insecure-resistant group (N = 5): the mean elicited play score was 8.33; the mean instructed play score was 14.83; and the mean executive capacity score was 0.20. For the insecure-disorganised group (N = 3): the mean elicited play score was 9.00; the mean instructed play score was 13.00; and the mean executive capacity score was 0.12.

Assessment of response to pretence suggestions

The executive capacity score provides a quantitative measure of how the level of sophistication of symbolic play is affected by instruction from an experimenter. In order to establish whether there were any qualitative differences between the securely and insecurely attached children's responses to instruction, the play sessions were subjected to further analysis. A child's response to being instructed to perform a specific act (see Table 5.1) was placed in one of six categories:

(1) *Ignore, continue irrelevant play*—the child ignores the experimenter's instruction and continues or begins a sequence of non-symbolic play;

(2) *Ignore, continue pretend play*—the child ignores the experimenter's instruction and continues the sequence of pretence that he or she had begun in the elicited condition;

(3) *Attempt, focus on representational toy*—the child responds to the experimenter's suggestion, but focuses exclusively on the representational toy (the doll or car), ignoring the junk object;

(4) *Attempt, focus on junk object*—the child responds to the experimenter's suggestion, but focuses exclusively on the junk object, ignoring the representational toy;

(5) *Succeed*—the child responds to the experimenter's suggestion and succeeds in performing the required sequence;

(6) *Hesitation or anxiety*—the child hesitates unduly, or seems anxious, perhaps retreating to his or her mother. This hesitation or anxiety appears to be caused not merely by the child being

uncertain of how to use the objects to comply with the experimenter's instruction.

These six response-to-pretence-suggestion categories were both exhaustive and exclusive.

The raw scores for each of the six response categories were converted into proportional scores by dividing by nine (the total number of play episodes; see Table 5.1). The mean proportional number of responses assigned to each of the response-to-pretence-suggestion categories for the two attachment and two SES groups are shown in Table 5.3. Only one child was deemed to have scored in the *Hesitation or anxiety* category; this child was from the secure group. Using mean rank scores, statistical tests showed that the securely attached children scored higher than their insecure peers on the categories *Attempt, focus on junk object* and *Succeed* (4 and 5), and lower than the insecure group on the categories *Ignore, continue irrelevant play, Ignore, continue pretend play* and *Attempt, focus on representational toy* (1, 2, and 3). The differences between the secure and insecure groups were apparently not a result of one group showing greater hesitation or anxiety which impaired their performance. In addition, status 1 children were significantly more likely than those of status 2 to ignore the experimenter's suggestions and engage in irrelevant play (category 1). No further differences were found between the higher and lower SES groups on any of the remaining response-to-pretence-suggestion categories.

TABLE 5.3
Mean proportional scores for each of the response-to-pretence-suggestion categories as a function of security of attachment and SES

	Attachment classification		SES	
	Secure (n = 26)	Insecure (n = 17)	Status 1 (n = 16)	Status 2 (n = 27)
Ignore, continue irrelevant play	0.04 (0.05)	0.18 (0.23)	0.15 (0.16)	0.05 (0.15)
Ignore, continue pretend play	0.06 (0.09)	0.29 (0.13)	0.16 (0.17)	0.14 (0.15)
Attempt, focus representational toy	0.04 (0.09)	0.11 (0.13)	0.07 (0.11)	0.07 (0.11)
Attempt, focus junk object	0.09 (0.12)	0.01 (0.03)	0.06 (0.10)	0.06 (0.11)
Succeed	0.77 (0.19)	0.40 (0.21)	0.56 (0.24)	0.67 (0.27)

Standard deviations are shown in brackets

For the three insecure attachment categories, the mean proportional scores were as follows:

	insecure-avoidant	insecure-resistant	insecure-disorganised
Ignore, continue irrelevant play	0.19	0.25	0.04
Ignore, continue pretend play	0.26	0.31	0.32
Aattempt, focus on representational toy	0.12	0.08	0.20
Attempt, focus on junk object	0.02	0.00	0.00
Succeed	0.40	0.36	0.44

The results of Study Three showed that: (1) there was no difference in the mean levels of *elicited* pretend play between the secure and insecure groups; (2) securely attached children benefited more from external suggestion and showed a greater difference between the level of play reached under the elicited and instructed play conditions than the insecure group; (3) compared with their insecurely attached peers, securely attached children had greater executive capacity scores. These results are therefore in the *opposite* direction to those of Belsky et al. (1984), who found that *in*securely attached children benefited more from the experimenter's intervention. The results of Study Three are, however, consistent with those of Slade (1987b), who found that securely attached children's play benefited more from maternal involvement, despite there being no differences between the secure and insecure groups in solo symbolic play. Compared with the children in the insecure group, upon being instructed to perform a specific play act, securely attached children in Study Three: (1) were more likely to succeed in following the experimenter's suggestion; (2) if they failed, were more likely to attempt the instructed activity by focusing on the junk object, not the representational toy; and (3) were less likely to ignore the experimenter's suggestion by involving themselves in other types of symbolic or non-symbolic play. These differences between the secure and insecure groups were neither a function of SES nor of the insecure children's greater hesitation or anxiety in the test situation. The results of Study Three thus extend Slade's (1987b) findings, in showing that the benefits of social collaboration enjoyed by securely attached children are not limited to interactions with their mothers.

These results suggest that children who are insecurely attached do not simply catch up with the performance of their securely attached peers in a structured pretend play situation. In contrast to Belsky et al.'s study of children between 12 and 18 months, by the time children have reached 2½ years of age, there are no attachment-related differences in their ability spontaneously to pretend using a set of objects. But this is not to say that securely attached children have lost the advantage which they showed at early ages; their superiority is now manifested in their ability to adapt a sequence of pretence in order to take into account the perspective of another person.

SECURITY OF ATTACHMENT AND SYMBOLIC ABILITIES

How do the results of Study Three tally with my earlier characterisation of the securely attached child? We know that the greater executive capacity scores of the securely attached children on the symbolic play task are not due to their greater capability in imaginative play, since there were no differences between the secure and insecure groups on elicited play at this age. We also know that the insecure group were more likely to continue with the play sequence that they had devised (rather than adapt the sequence to incorporate the experimenter's suggestion) in the instructed condition. Moreover, we know that securely attached children established their superiority in the instructed play condition, not by virtue of their own imaginations, but because they were able to use the imaginative suggestions of the experimenter to enrich their sequences of pretence. In other words, the securely attached children in Study Three were using the experimenter's suggestions as a resource to extend the scope of their play. This ability may reflect differences in *social flexibility* between the secure and insecure groups, since securely attached children may have been more socially responsive, and therefore better able to "tune in" to what the experimenter was suggesting, perhaps even construing her as a playmate.

Why might securely attached children be more capable of accommodating external suggestions for play? One explanation is that this kind of social responsiveness has been fostered in previous interactions with their caregivers. Such a suggestion would be consistent with my interpretation of the findings of Study Two on linguistic acquisitional style. The securely attached children's propensity to acquire many object words and not to rely on frozen phrases suggests that they will have been exposed to different perspectives on the world from a very early age. Why? Because by talking about objects, rather than using language expressively, the child will have been exposed to an environment where the expression of different views about the same object within the "primordial sharing situation" (Werner and Kaplan, 1963) will be commonplace. Given the findings of Study Two, it is therefore not surprising that securely attached children in Study Three were better not only at recognising that the experimenter was offering an alternative perspective on how the objects could be used, but also in *taking up* this suggestion and using it to direct their play.

The notion that securely attached children may be better able to benefit from external involvement in play because of the types of interaction that have been encouraged by their mothers is supported by the findings of Slade (1987b). Slade reported that mothers of securely attached children tended to favour active participation in their children's play, whereas mothers who had insecure relationships with their children preferred to interact with them in more passive ways. Moreover, these differences were most evident when the mother was required to divide her attention. When they were involved in a conversation with the experimenter, Slade found that mothers in the insecure group virtually ignored their children. In contrast, the mothers in the secure group could maintain active engagement in their children's play while they talked to the experimenter. If securely attached children are thus accustomed to active maternal intervention in their play, then this may lead to them forming expectations about the function that other adults may serve within a play context.

The present conjectures are therefore two-fold. First, securely attached children are better able to benefit from external involvement in play because they are, in a sense, more "open" psychological systems: their options for behaviour are less foreclosed than those of their insecurely attached peers and they are more sensitive to influences from the social setting. To return to a point made earlier (p.81), it seems that the differences between the secure and insecure groups in symbolic play become more subtle as they get older. Securely attached toddlers have lost the advantage in overall sophistication of solo play that they enjoyed in infancy, but their greater self-efficacy is now manifested in their ability to respond to the play suggestions of others. The second conjecture is that it is possible that the mothers in the secure group are partly responsible for their children's greater social flexibility, since their style of interaction within the context of play may have engendered in them certain expectations about how others may act as play collaborators.

We are thus led back to the earlier consideration of how factors such as maternal sensitivity might account for differences observed between securely and insecurely attached children. In Chapter Two, I discussed the necessity to distinguish between different ways in which mothers could demonstrate their sensitivity to their children. To recap, sensitivity within the emotional realm may be associated with the establishment of a secure attachment relationship, and sensitivity in the cognitive realm may be responsible for securely attached children's greater self-efficacy. This notion of self-efficacy was in turn used to explain the security-based differences in search behaviour and language acquisition reported in Studies One and Two. One can also use this notion of self-efficacy to account for the differences seen between the secure and insecure groups in Study Three. Given that these differences were only found during the more challenging context of instructed play, we may suppose that securely attached children's superior performance was due to their greater ability to act upon the suggestions of the experimenter.

The results of Study Three may provide us with a further clue to the cause of securely attached children's superior performance on tasks of this nature. It may be that, by interacting with the child in a sensitive manner within the cognitive realm, mothers of securely attached children not only instill in them a sense of self-efficacy, but give them a template for interacting with other people. The existence of such a template is extremely difficult to prove, but in later chapters I will argue that it provides a useful construct for accounting for security-related differences. Differences in maternal sensitivity, on the other hand, should be readily observable. Before I report a study to investigate the relationship between security of attachment and maternal sensitivity, it is necessary to introduce certain theoretical concepts which will serve as the basis for my subsequent investigations.

THEORETICAL CONSIDERATIONS

It has often been noted that some kind of responsive interaction with others is essential for an understanding of one's own efficacy. For example, Mead (1934) suggested that mere exposure to other perspectives in a social context will lead to an ability to represent and act upon the views and attitudes of others. On such a view, one would not predict any differences between attachment groups, since all children, whatever their attachment classification, will have been exposed to the requisite type of social interaction. That said, it may be that these other "perspectives" need to be presented in a form which the child is able to understand and assimilate. My conjecture, to be spelled out in the remainder of this book, is that it is the mothers in the secure group who tend to be able reliably to identify this appropriate level of interaction and instruction. Such mothers will therefore be better able to recognise their child's current level of ability, and to target interaction in a way that maximises the child's chances of comprehension. By maintaining sensitive and flexible interaction with their children, these mothers will provide greater opportunities for exchange of information and knowledge.

Vygotsky (1978) identified the most effective type of tutoring as that which concentrated on the child's *zone of proximal development*, defined as "the distance between the actual developmental level as determined by independent problem solving and the level of potential development as determined through problem solving under adult guidance or in collaboration with more capable peers" (p.86). The measures taken in Study Three and in Belsky et al.'s (1984) and Slade's (1987b) studies have certain commonalities with Vygotsky's notion of the zone of proximal development (ZPD), inasmuch as they compared children's levels of solo performance with performance after adult intervention.

Vygotsky's ideas on play may also help us to understand the apparent contradiction between the results of Study Three and those of Belsky et al. (1984). Vygotsky (1933) claimed that "in play activity thought is separated from objects, and actions arise from ideas rather than from things" (p.546). Belsky et al.'s children were apparently too young to have begun to divorce the meaning of an object from its appearance, and in any case, the materials used to elicit pretend play were confined to miniatures of adult objects. However, the children in Study Three were old enough to recognise that the junk objects could be other than they are. It is not unreasonable to suppose that securely attached children's superiority in instructed play stems from their greater social flexibility, manifested in their ability to divorce perceptual meaning from symbolic meaning using not only their own ideas, but also those of another person.

NOTE

1.   The results of this study are published in full as: Meins, E., & Russell, J. (1997). Security and symbolic play: The relation between security of attachment and executive capacity. *British Journal of Developmental Psychology, 15,* 63–77.

CHAPTER SIX

Security of attachment and maternal sensitivity within a tutoring context

> [Instruction in the ZPD] calls to life in the child, awakens and puts in motion an entire series of internal processes of development. These processes are at the time possible only in the sphere of interaction with those surrounding the child and in collaboration with companions, but in the internal course of development they eventually become the internal properties of the child. (Vygotsky, 1956, p.450)

In considering the child's potential to develop, Vygotsky (1956) maintained that "we can take stock not only of today's completed process of development, not only the cycles that are already concluded and done, not only the processes of maturation that are completed; we can also take stock of processes that are now in the state of coming into being, that are only ripening or developing" (pp.447-8). He believed that the ZPD does not innately exist for each individual child; instead "instruction creates the zone of proximal development" (ibid., p.450). Furthermore, as the quotation at the beginning of the chapter illustrates, instruction is only beneficial if it is geared to a level ahead of the child's development, although Vygotsky argued that this upper limit will be fixed by the child's intellectual potential.

So far I have considered how securely attached children's apparent superiority across a range of tasks is dependent upon a particular type of infant-mother interaction. If such differences in interaction do indeed exist, it should be possible to measure them within a tutoring situation. Specifically, it may be that securely attached children's superiority on these tasks stems from their mothers' ability to interact with them within the ZPD, which will in turn be related to their sensitivity to the gap between their children's current and potential levels of functioning.

MATERNAL TUTORING STRATEGIES

Influenced by the work of Bernstein (1961), researchers in the 1960s investigated the differences between middle and working class mothers' ability to teach their children (e.g. Bee et al., 1969; Hess & Shipman, 1965). Bernstein emphasised the importance of maternal speech in shaping the child's cognitive and linguistic development, suggesting that there were two linguistic modes used for communication and organisation of experience. Working class parents, he argued, were more likely to use a "public" language mode, whereas middle class parents used a "formal" mode. This distinction in speech between the classes was based on measures such as syntactic complexity and flexibility in grammatical construction, as well as speech content. The middle class parents were found to be more likely to use syntactically complicated sentence structures and, rather than dictate to their children, would use reason in order to make them comply with an instruction. Concern with such class differences in maternal language led to a considerable amount of research into the teaching methods used by working and middle class mothers. Hess and Shipman (1965) reported that the strategies used by middle class mothers in teaching their 4-year-olds how to draw using an *Etch-a-Sketch* toy were more focused and efficient than those used by working class mothers. In support of Bernstein's contention that maternal language affected the child's intellectual development, Hess and Shipman found that maternal teaching strategy was as good a predictor of the child's cognitive development as the child's IQ.

Bee et al. (1969) explored in more detail the dimensions of mother-child interactions that may be responsible for the child's cognitive development, using children who were part of the American Head Start Program. They secretly observed the mother and child in a "waiting room" situation, after which the mother-infant pair took part in a collaborative problem-solving task. Bee et al. found that, in the waiting room situation, middle class mothers were less controlling, less disapproving and gave their children more information and attention than the working class mothers. On the tutoring task, Bee et al. argued that the most effective teaching strategy was characterised by a majority of commands at a low level of specificity and a lack of physical intervention. The authors concluded that "middle class mothers, regardless of the situation, used more instruction, less physical intrusion, less negative feedback, and were generally more in tune with the child's individual needs and qualities" (1969, p.732). At first glance, this conclusion seems to be reasonable: one should encourage children, make general comments and not overwhelm them with too much physical intervention. But if we look more closely at the types of task a child needs to learn how to perform, we can see that there will be many instances when this approach will not be optimal. For example, consider a child who is trying to build a toy from some pieces of Lego: he or she will be able to accomplish some parts of the task easily, but may begin to run into difficulties when more complex or dextrous operations are required. When such difficulties arise, the most effective method of instruction would be for the mother or tutor to use more specific, directive instructions and perhaps physically demonstrate how to perform certain actions. The work of Wood and colleagues in the 1970s (Wood, Bruner, & Ross, 1976; Wood & Middleton, 1975; Wood, Wood, & Middleton, 1978) represented a marked improvement on the early tutoring studies, since these authors analysed a mother's behaviour *within a framework of success/failure feedback from the child.*

In their seminal study, Wood et al. (1976) evaluated the efficacy of an experimenter's tutoring style in teaching a group of 3- to 5-year olds how to construct a pyramid from a series of interconnecting pieces. On the basis of previous findings (e.g. Clinchy, 1974; Olson, 1966, 1970), Wood et al. hypothesised that children should recognise a goal or sub-goal of a task before being able to produce the operational sequence to achieve it. They argued that the most effective method of tutoring is one which focuses on this recognition-production gap, highlighting the important role played by the tutor's ability to use feedback from the child's performance in achieving this focus. This led to the definition of one of the central concepts in the field of tutoring strategies: *scaffolding*, which consists of "the adult 'controlling' those elements of the task that are initially beyond the learner's capacity, thus permitting him to concentrate upon and complete only those elements that are within his range of competence" (Wood et al., 1976, p.90). The level of specificity of the tutor's interventions is thus contingent on the child's previous success or failure.

Wood et al. found that a number of other factors, in addition to the use of feedback, were important in scaffolding the child's performance on a task. First, it appeared that the tutor's use of encouraging and reassuring comments helped the child to maintain the motivation to complete the task successfully. The tutor could also scaffold the child's performance by drawing attention to various critical features and reiterating useful strategies, since these comments provided the child with a more general framework for approaching the task. Finally, in order for demonstration to be of use in the scaffolding process, the tutor must ensure that the child is involved if a step is being demonstrated, and that the demonstrated action is assimilable.

To what extent is this optimal strategy adopted by mothers? Wood and Middleton (1975) investigated the teaching strategies employed by mothers using the same task as Wood et al. (1976), and found that some mothers did indeed scaffold their children's performance, concentrating on the recognition-production gap. Wood and Middleton identified the ideal level of intervention as being one above that at which the child is already performing, referring to this discrepancy between actual and potential competence as the *region of sensitivity to instruction*. Clearly, this construct is similar to the ZPD, since both are defined in terms of actual and potential levels of performance (see p.91 for Vygotsky's definition of the ZPD). If a mother is able to identify her child's level of cognitive ability, she will be better able to make comments and suggestions which will be simple enough to be understood, but sufficiently advanced for the child to work out the general rules that need to be followed to complete the task. As Wood and Middleton stated, "[the mother] should not want to see [her child] 'swamped' by too many possibilities, but neither should she want to stifle his performance by doing too much herself" (1975, p.182). Once again, the role played by feedback from the child's performance was deemed crucial in establishing a tutoring strategy which was contingent on the child's needs. Within a contingent tutoring framework, if the child succeeds in following an instruction, subsequent ones should be less explicit, leaving the child more "work" to do in reaching the solution. Conversely, if the child has difficulty in following an instruction, the mother should give more explicit cues, "thus confronting the child with less uncertainty and a greater probability of some task success" (ibid., p.190).

The work of Wood and his colleagues has been important in defining the optimal teaching method in a problem-solving situation, but it did not attempt to characterise any other similarities amongst those mothers who were "good tutors". As I have argued elsewhere, (Meins, 1997), the qualities which appear to be important in establishing scaffolding relate to features of the parent-child relationship, rather than being character-istics of the child or parent as individuals. Since one of the central arguments of this book is that caregivers of securely attached children are sensitive to their current levels of ability, adapting their interactions to take into account the child's needs, we should look for attachment-related differences in the caregiver's ability to tutor her child within the ZPD.

TUTORING STRATEGIES AND SECURITY OF ATTACHMENT

Previous research into maternal tutoring strategies has typically involved collaboration on a novel task, which the child will never have performed before. The optimal teaching strategy involves the tutor reliably identifying the child's level of competence, updating this assessment on the basis of feedback from the child's performance throughout the task, and altering the specificity of subsequent instructions where necessary. In order for the tutor or mother to identify how capable the child is of performing a novel task, she must first allow the child to experiment and set the base level of competence for the task. Therefore, the first step must be for the mother to take a back seat and give the child full responsibility for getting on with the task. Of course, in order for the mother to be able to do this, the child must be autonomous and confident enough to "have a go". Although the study reported in this chapter does not address this issue directly, there would nevertheless seem to be an immediate reason for predicting security-based differences in such circumstances, given the characterisation of securely attached children as having a greater sense of self-efficacy than their insecurely attached peers.

It has been difficult to demonstrate that the use of optimal teaching strategies leads to general advancement in cognitive development, beyond the scope of the skills required for completing the particular tasks used in tutoring studies. For example, the studies performed by Wood and colleagues using the pyramid task (Wood et al., 1976; Wood & Middleton, 1975) included a post-test condition, in which the child had to build the pyramid without the adult's help. However, this post-test performance is a highly specific measure of the effect of contingent tutoring on cognitive performance, and from these results, we do not know whether the skills learnt in this context were generalisable or long-lasting. Part of the problem may be that the link between tutoring strategies and task performance may be mediated by child-centred factors such as self-efficacy, confidence and task engagement. There is good reason to suppose that mothers of securely attached children may be better at fostering these qualities in their children. For example, Londerville and Main (1981) reported that, on a collaborative task, mothers of securely attached children intervened more gently and instructed their children using "warmer tones" than their counterparts in the insecure group. These differences in interaction were associated with the securely attached children's relatively greater compliance and cooperation on the task.

As discussed in earlier chapters, mothers of securely attached children tend to be more consistent in their patterns of mothering (Isabella, 1993), and are more sensitive, accepting, cooperative and available for dealing with their children's requests and needs (Ainsworth, Bell, & Stayton, 1971). This greater awareness of their children's requirements, especially in the cognitive realm, may mean that mothers of securely attached children will be more likely to scaffold their performance in a tutoring situation, and nurture in the child a sense of responsibility for the task. Diaz, Neal, and Vachio (1991) asserted that this transfer of responsibility to the child is augmented if the tutor uses encouragement and reassurance. Diaz et al. investigated mothers' abilities to transfer responsibility for selective attention and sequencing tasks to their 3-year-olds in both a high risk (due to previous abuse and/or neglect) and low risk sample. Their results showed that mothers in the high risk group were less likely to praise and encourage their children, to use questions and statements requesting their children to take responsibility for part of the task, or to help them form relevant conceptual representations or plans. Diaz et al. concluded that an "affective-motivational" variable, often embedded in positive attributions of children's competence, might be the most important mediating variable in the ... relation between social interaction and cognitive development" (1991, p.104). Since children from such high risk samples tend to be insecurely attached (e.g. Cicchetti, 1990; Cicchetti & Barnet, 1991; Crittenden & Ainsworth, 1989; Egeland & Sroufe, 1981; Lamb, Gaensbauer, Malkin, & Schultz, 1985), this could be taken as indirect evidence of a link between security of attachment and maternal tutoring styles. More importantly, in light of the evidence cited in this book so far, one would assume that the "affective-motivational" tutoring style posited by Diaz et al. would be most likely to be characteristic of secure attachment relationships.

If it is the case that mothers of securely attached children tend to engage them in interactions which are sensitive to the gap between their actual and potential levels of performance, it should be possible to demonstrate this sensitivity experimentally. This is what was attempted in the study reported below. The prediction was that mothers of securely attached children will be more effective tutors in the following respects: (1) in giving didactic suggestions that are neither too far beyond nor too close to the child's current level of functioning; (2) in being encouraging rather than punitive; and (3) in directing the child's play sensitively by using feedback from the child's performance to alter the specificity of subsequent interventions.

STUDY FOUR[1]

The subjects were 37 (12 girls, 25 boys) of the original children who had participated in Studies One, Two and Three. The average age of the children was 3 years, 1 month (range: 2 years, 11 months to 3 years, 2 months). Of the 37 subjects, 22 were securely attached, 8 were insecure-avoidant, 5 were insecure-resistant and 2 were insecure-disorganised.

Given that numerous studies have reported differences in maternal tutoring strategies associated with SES in conjunction with occupational status and educational attainment (e.g. Bee et al., 1969; Diaz et al., 1991; Laosa, 1980), the measure of these children's SES was perhaps of greater importance to the questions addressed in Study Four than to those in the three previously reported studies. To recap, this SES measure was based on: maternal education, mother's present/previous occupation and father's occupation (Mueller & Parcel, 1981). That is, a family was considered to be (1) "status 1" if the father and mother had manual/unskilled jobs and the mother had left school at the minimum leaving age, and (2) "status 2" if the mother and father were in professional or managerial positions and the mother had either gone on to further education or had qualified to do so. No problematic combinations arose in the sample.

Of the 37 subjects, 13 (7 from the secure and 6 from the insecure group) were classified as status 1 and 24 (15 from the secure and 9 from the insecure) were classified as status 2. There was no relationship between SES and security of attachment for the children who took part in Study Four.

Maternal teaching strategies

The children were tested in the department's developmental laboratory, apart from five of the child-mother pairs, who were tested at home. All of the sessions were video-taped.

The child was presented with a stack of eight *Polydron* squares and a model box which had already been constructed (see Fig. 6.1). As Fig. 6.1. shows, two of these squares can only be fitted together when they are both in the correct orientation, due to the configuration of the gaps and joining sections on their sides. Consequently, it is sometimes necessary to turn one of the squares over, so that the joining section of one square's side will be aligned with the corresponding gap in the side of the second square. The experimenter demonstrated to the mother and child how the squares fitted together, telling the mother: "The idea is that this will be too difficult for [name] to manage on his/her own, so you can give as much or as little help as you like". The experimenter then said to the child: "[Name], I'd like you to build me a box just like

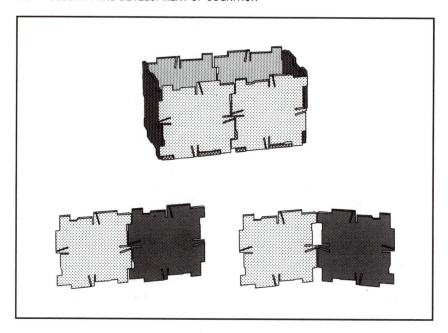

FIG. 6.1. The apparatus used in the box construction task.

this one using these squares. You see, the box has different coloured sides and a different coloured bottom, so build one just like this". The mother and child were allowed to work on constructing the box for as long as they wished, and the session only ended if the mother and child gave up or if the box was completed.

This task was used to obtain a measure of the levels of verbal instruction and physical intervention used by the mother in a teaching context. Certain aspects of the scoring procedure used in the present study were adapted from Bee et al. (1969) and Wood and Middleton (1975). Each intervention the mother made was scored in two ways. First, the content and form of mothers' verbal interventions was assessed: e.g. question or non-question, positive or negative feedback. The total number of physical interventions made by each mother was also measured, and this category was sub-divided in terms of whether interventions were spontaneous or requested by the child. Second, the level of specificity of all interventions was assessed: levels of specificity ranged from general comments, e.g. "Look at the box", "Let's start with the bottom" (Level 1 specificity), to demonstration of an operation by the mother without the involvement of the child (Level 5 specificity). In Table 6.1 examples are given of comments indicative of these levels of specificity.

TABLE 6.1
Example of comments indicating the five levels of specificity on the box construction task

Level of specificity	Description and typical comments
Level 1	Orienting suggestions, focusing strategies, general rules and comments, e.g. "Look at the box", "Let's start with the bottom", "You have to turn the pieces round"
Level 2	Suggestions about specific pieces, locations, or actions, but not combinations of the three, e.g. "Find a red one like this", "Push the pieces together"
Level 3	Solutions—suggestions indicating which piece should be used and where to put it, e.g. "That piece fits in here"
Level 4	Physical help—the mother physically aids the child in completing a section, e.g. holding one square in place whilst the child attaches another
Level 5	Demonstration—the mother performs an operation by herself

First, the mother-child dyad's performance in constructing the box was analysed for the specificity of the mother's verbal instructions (levels 1-5 in Table 6.1) and the amount of maternal physical intervention. Each child-mother pair received scores for the number of (1) questions, (2) positive feedback and (3) negative feedback statements as proportions of the total number of verbal instructions given during the task. The numbers of requested nonverbal and spontaneous nonverbal interventions by each mother were scored as proportions of her total number of physical interventions during the task.

The mean proportional scores for the categories which showed a significant difference between the secure and insecure group are shown in Table 6.2. No differences were found between the secure and insecure groups in the proportion of questions used or on the index of *general* non-verbal intervention. There were significant differences between the two SES groups on the measures of positive and negative feedback. Status 1 mothers used proportionately more negative feedback comments (a mean of 0.10 compared with 0.05 for the status 2 mothers), and proportionately less positive feedback statements (a mean of 0.11 compared with 0.20 for mothers in the status 2 group).

Secondly, the *temporal pattern* of the mother's suggestions and interventions was analysed. This scoring procedure provided a minute-by-minute account of the amount and level of intervention used by the mother and the corresponding success/failure of her child in complying, and was used to assess a mother's sensitivity to feedback.

TABLE 6.2
Categories on which there were significant differences in mean proportional
scores between the secure and insecure groups

Category	Mean proportional score		
	Secure group	Insecure group	
Positive feedback	0.21 (0.12)	0.12 (0.08)	$p < 0.05$
Negative feedback	0.04 (0.04)	0.11 (0.10)	$p < 0.005$
Spontaneous non-verbal intervention	0.18 (0.08)	0.24 (0.05)	$p < 0.05$
Requested non-verbal intervention	0.04 (0.05)	0.01 (0.03)	$p. < 0.05$

Standard deviations are shown in brackets

Sensitivity to feedback

The mother's sensitivity to feedback was defined in terms of her ability
to change the level of specificity of her suggestion in response to feedback
on the child's ability to follow each instruction successfully. The number
of times a mother used the feedback from her child's performance to alter
the level of specificity of intervention (levels 1-5 above) was calculated.
A mother's successful use of feedback to change the specificity of her
instruction was coded according to the following rules. In order for use
of feedback to be successful:

1. If the child succeeds at a given level of specificity, the next
   instruction should be given *at the same level or at a lower level* of
   specificity;
2. (a) if the child fails at a given level of specificity, the next
   instruction should be given *at a higher level* of specificity;
   (b) if the child fails at a given level of specificity, the next
   instruction should be *no more than two levels* above the previous
   level of specificity.

Parts 1 and 2(a) are equivalent to Wood et al.'s (1978) contingency rule,
with one exception: that the permitted rise in specificity in the present
study was limited to two levels above the previous instruction. This was
done since a jump from a Level 1 instruction to giving the child physical
help or demonstrating the action was not considered to be a contingent,
optimal teaching strategy.[2]

A mother's sensitivity to feedback score was taken to be the number
of appropriate changes made in the specificity of intervention (according
to the above rules) as a proportion of her total number of interventions.
The mean sensitivity to feedback score for the secure group mothers was

0.60 compared to 0.41 for the mothers in the insecure group. This represented a difference at the 0.0025 level of significance. There were no differences between the two SES groups on this measure of sensitivity to feedback.

For the three insecure attachment groups, the mean sensitivity scores were as follows: the insecure-avoidant group's mean (N = 8) was 0.49; the insecure-resistant group's mean (N = 5) was 0.39; and the insecure-disorganised group's mean (N = 2) was 0.35. The similarity of these means does, however, mask some interesting differences between the three insecure groups, which are discussed in greater detail below.

The results of Study Four showed that, in comparison with their counterparts in the insecurely attached group, mothers of securely attached children: (1) gave their children more positive and less negative feedback; (2) were significantly less likely to use spontaneous non-verbal intervention; (3) were more likely to intervene physically when asked to do so by the child (requested non-verbal intervention); and (4) pitched their interventions at an appropriate level, given the child's previous success or failure.

In addition, the results of the present study largely supported those of previous research into the relationship between maternal tutoring strategies and SES (e.g. Bee et al., 1969; Diaz et al., 1991; Laosa, 1980). That is, mothers from the higher SES group used more positive, encouraging feedback and less negative feedback in interactions with their children. On these factors, the mothers in the secure group therefore show the same characteristics as those in the higher SES group, which raises the suspicion that the observed differences between the secure and insecure groups may merely be a reflection of SES. However, there was no overall relationship between security of attachment and SES, and the differences found between the secure and insecure groups on the other measures of intervention (spontaneous and requested non-verbal intervention) and maternal sensitivity to feedback appear to be independent of SES.

To move on to a more qualitative analysis, mothers in the secure group tended to demonstrate those types of intervention which Wood et al. (1976) identified as constituting scaffolding. These mothers were more willing to allow their children to go at their own pace and were less likely to be critical when the child inevitably made mistakes. They seemed to act as a kind of mediator between the task and their children, asking open but directive questions in order to help the children ask the right questions of themselves. They were more encouraging and responsive to the child's requests for help, and when these mothers did physically intervene, help was attuned to the child's current level of understanding: too much help and children may lose engagement in the task and their autonomy may be muted; too little and they are left floundering. Mothers in the secure group reassured and supported their children in their efforts and reiterated strategies which the children had previously employed successfully. For example, some mothers reminded their children that the squares may need turning over in order for them to fit together.

Mothers in the secure group were also more likely to demonstrate greater sensitivity in their physical interventions. As Wood et al. (1976) noted, some children will sometimes need to be shown what to do, since they are unable to "unpack" a verbal instruction to achieve the appropriate sequence of operations. Implicit in "showing" a child how to perform some action is the notion that the child will be involved in the proceedings; indeed he or she may even have asked for this kind of assistance. The analysis of physical intervention made in Study Four was interesting in this respect, in that although there were no differences between the *overall* amount of physical intervention by the mothers in the secure and insecure groups, when this category was subdivided into *requested* physical intervention and *spontaneous* physical intervention, significant differences between the secure and insecure groups emerged. Mothers in the secure groups were more likely to intervene physically after their children requested them to do so, whereas mothers in the insecure group were more likely to intervene physically without any such requests from their children. Once again, these differences between the secure and insecure groups could not be explained in terms of SES. Moreover, if mothers in the secure group demonstrated an operation to their children, they tended to do so in a way that actively involved them in the proceedings, and explained what they were doing in a way that the children could understand. This kind of behaviour is illustrated by the following example:

Mother   Let's see if we can remember how to put these together, because they weren't that easy. You have a little go first. (*Encourages responsibility*)

Child tries, but one square is the wrong way round.

Child   I can't do it. (*Request for help*)
Mother   Well, you'll be able to in a minute. (*Reassurance*) (Mother turns square over.) Ahh. Turn it over and try again. There. Just push it down. (Helps. Success.) How does that look? That's fine! (*Positive feedback*) What we should do now ... What side do you want to do next? (*Encourages responsibility*) The green, two blues and the red (pointing to model box).

Child   I think I want to do the green now.

Mother   Sometimes, if it doesn't work, it's worth turning it over and trying it the other way. (Points to the green square) (*Reiterating previously successful strategy*)

Child turns the square round.

Mother   Lift it up and actually turn it over.

Child complies.

Mother   I think you'll find that will fit. (*Reassurance*)

Success.

Mother   Oh great! That's the idea. (*Positive feedback*) So sometimes we have to turn them over to make them fit. (*Reiterating previously successful strategy*)

In contrast to this pattern of tutoring exemplified by the secure group mothers, the behaviour of the mothers in the insecure group was found to be non-contingent with their children's performance in one of two ways: (1) underestimating the child's ability; and (2) overestimating the child's ability. Mothers who showed the first type of tutoring pattern tended not to give their children sufficient time to react to one suggestion before making another, and, on anecdotal evidence, often seemed to be more concerned with working out *for themselves* how the task could be accomplished. These mothers therefore did not seem to be able to pitch the level or timing of intervention within the ZPD, and tended to violate two of Wood et al.'s "rules of scaffolding" (see pp.95–96), since they did not try to involve their children in their demonstrations or make their comments comprehensible. The comments of these mothers often showed that they were aware of taking too active a role in the task, but they still persisted in physically intervening, which stifled their children's performance. One mother, for example, remarked that this was "a game for mummies"! The following extract illustrates a typical exchange between a child and his "underestimating" mother.

Child picks up two yellow squares.

Mother   Shall we make the bottom first? Can you make two of those go together? And then we can build the bottom of the box. (*Instructions in quick succession*)

Child tries to fit the squares together.

Mother   Mmm. I don't know how this works, this.

Mother lifts child's hands off the squares (*Discourages responsibility*)

Mother   Let me ... Let mummy see if she can do it. (*Discourages responsibility*)

Mother turns squares around.

Mother   Shall we turn it round and try this side? Yes? (Snaps squares together herself.) Has that snapped together? Yes, that's snapped together. Well done. Now, we've got to do a side of the box, all right? Using the two red bits. So can you give me the two red bits? (*Instructions in quick succession*)
Child   Here's the red bits.

Child picks up the red squares and tries to fit them together.

Mother   That's not going to work is it? (*Negative feedback*) ... We'll have to lift them up a bit, won't we? (*Incomprehensible comment*)
Child   Why?
Mother   Cos, em, it'd be easier, wouldn't it? Unless they push together. (Mother joins the squares.) There, they do push together. Now what we have to do is stick those yellow bits onto this red bit. And that we do ... Oh dearie, dearie me. (*Incomprehensible comment*)

Mother looks at model box

Child   What's a dearie?
Mother   (Laughs.) Mummy just says this is a very difficult thing, and you'll be clever if you can do this. So I want you to help me (*Encourages responsibility*) (Child looks away) and not wriggle around and look at the toys over there. (*Negative feedback*)

The second type of tutoring pattern seen in the insecure group mothers was that of overestimating their children's ability to perform the task. By adopting this kind of strategy, the mother gave her child very little guidance and help, whilst seemingly expecting an optimal performance and a high degree of compliance from the child. Since even the most skilful children in the sample needed guidance on some parts of the task, this overestimating strategy tended to result in the child losing interest because he or she was unable to enjoy any success. In turn, this led to children becoming disillusioned with the box construction, which tended to result in the mothers using more negative feedback in an attempt to prevent the child from being inattentive. It should be noted that these mothers used lots of low specificity instructions, which was something which Hess and Shipman (1965) and Bee et al. (1969) asserted was part of a good maternal tutoring pattern. This serves to show that such generalisations are not the most fruitful way of categorising tutoring strategies, and that it is more important to take into consideration the initial competence of the child and the difficulty of the task.

These overestimating mothers were the group most likely to violate rule 2(b) of the sensitivity to instruction measure.[3] However, a high degree of maternal physical intervention is not surprising in such contexts, since if the child cannot begin to attempt the task, and is not given any explicit verbal instructions or assimilable physical demonstrations, the only way for any of the box to be constructed is for the mother to do it herself. Some anecdotal evidence is interesting with respect to this point. It appeared that, like the mothers in the underestimating group, overestimating mothers did not simultaneously explain or justify their actions whilst demonstrating an operation. But unlike the underestimating mothers, this group seemed unaware of their over-involvement in the collaboration task. An example of a typical exchange between a child and an underestimating mother is given in Note 2 (p.109).

Descriptive data from the three insecure attachment groups are interesting, since they suggest that the type of insecure attachment may be related to the type of tutoring strategy employed by the mother. Specifically, mothers in the insecure-avoidant group tended to adopt an underestimating tutoring strategy, with 6 of the 7 mothers in this group showing this pattern of behaviour. The example of the insecure dyad's exchange given above is from an insecure-avoidant dyad, and typifies the very specific comments made by these mothers. This finding of quite high levels of intrusion in the avoidant group is consistent with their observed patterns of interaction in infancy. For example, several researchers have reported that mothers of avoidant infants overwhelm them with too much intrusive intervention (Belsky, Rovine, & Taylor, 1984; Isabella & Belsky, 1991; Lewis & Feiring, 1989; Smith & Pederson, 1988). Moreover, Isabella (1993) defined the rejecting behaviour of mothers in the avoidant group in terms of their propensity physically to control and interfere with the infant. No such clear patterns of behaviour appeared to be associated with the insecure-resistant or insecure-disorganised groups.

THE CHILD AS AN ACTIVE PARTICIPANT IN THE TUTORING PROCESS

The results of Study Four add to the body of knowledge that we have on the development of these groups of securely and insecurely attached children. Since their security of attachment was assessed at 11 or 13 months of age (see Study One), there appears to be a distinct continuity of functioning in these infant-mother dyads from infancy through to early childhood. Thus, although the term scaffolding has been used primarily to refer to tutoring strategies, it may in fact be applicable to the secure group mothers' interactions with their children *in general*.

What implications do the results of Study Four and those reported in the previous chapters have for the future development of these securely and insecurely attached children? The results of Study Two highlighted differences in securely and insecurely attached children's linguistic acquisitional style, which I argued reflected the nature of communic- ative exchanges between securely attached children and their mothers, particularly the presentation of different perspectives within the context of object-centred interaction. In addition to these findings relating to language, we know that securely attached children are more autonomous and independent (e.g. Ainsworth et al., 1978), have greater ego strength (Lütkenhaus et al., 1985) and are better at incorporating the suggestions of an experimenter into a sequence of symbolic play (see Study Three). We also know from the results of Study Four that mothers of securely attached children interact with them within the ZPD, are sensitive to the fluctuating needs of their children in a tutoring context, and appear to see advantages in giving their children responsibility for some of the task. In essence, scaffolding the child's performance involves keeping the task within the ZPD, so that the child can continue to regulate his or her own behaviour. One could therefore argue that these mothers show a greater tendency to treat their children as "mental agents", taking into account their comments, actions and perspective on the task. The term I shall use to describe this ability in mothers is *mind-mindedness*, the correlates and consequences of which will be outlined in the final two chapters.

I have characterised the differences observed between the secure and insecure groups on the range of tasks reported in this book in terms of securely attached children's greater self-efficacy. It was suggested that this sense of self-efficacy arises because securely attached children's mothers are more likely to demonstrate mind-mindedness with their infants and interact with them in a sensitive manner from an early age. From the results of Study Three, I argued that such maternal sensitivity may provide the child with a template for interacting with others in collaborative contexts as well as a sense of self-efficacy. The greater sensitivity of the secure group mothers was demonstrated on a cognitive-based task in Study Four. It is not unreasonable to suppose that the different experiences of securely and insecurely attached children across this range of contexts might affect the development of the child's ability to represent the perspectives of others. Tasks which measure children's understanding of beliefs, and their role in determining behaviour, are an obvious way of testing this possibility, and this area is the focus of the final study to be reported in this book.

NOTES

1. The results of this study are published in full as: Meins, E. (1997). Security of attachment and maternal tutoring strategies: Interaction within the zone of proximal development. *British Journal of Developmental Psychology*, 15, 129–144.

2. The following extract clarifies this point: after several failures to follow the mother's instructions,

    Mother What do we need to do now? (Level 1)

    Child picks up a completed side of the box

    Mother Look. (Demonstrates snapping the two squares together.) (Level 5) There. What comes next? (Level 1)

    Thus, although the mother has obeyed rule 2(a), it is unlikely that the child will have benefited maximally from this kind of teaching strategy.

3. Rule 2(b): If the child fails at a given level of specificity, the next instruction should be no more than two levels above the previous level of specificity.

CHAPTER SEVEN

Security of attachment and the understanding of other minds

> We can acknowledge that children, like scientists, rely on analogy, while at the same time denying that they proceed to the formulation of a theory of mind. Skilled mind-reading ... calls for the imaginative resonance of the biographer rather than the theoretical postulates of the scientist. (Harris, 1991, p.302)

From the contribution of quite recent research, we know that an understanding of other minds is something which develops in the first three or four years of life. When children are as young as 2 years of age, they make verbal references to mental states, such as desires and perceptions (e.g. Bretherton & Beeghly, 1982; Shatz, Wellman, & Silber, 1983), and around their third birthday they begin to understand mental states relating to thinking and knowing (Bartsch & Wellman, 1989). Evidence for such sophisticated comprehension at such a young age led Wellman (1991) to describe 2-year-olds as "internal state theorists" who understand that people have different desires directed towards particular objects and states of affairs. However, children at this age still have problems comprehending other people's beliefs about aspects of the world.

The question of when children come to understand the beliefs of others has been the subject of countless studies and theories over recent years. The most well-founded conclusion of this ever-increasing body of research is that, some time around their fourth birthday, children come to understand that someone's false belief about a state of affairs can lead to inappropriate behaviour. This was first demonstrated in Wimmer and Perner's (1983) classic "unexpected transfer" task, which is centred around a boy called Maxi and his search for some chocolate. The child is told the story of how Maxi left his chocolate in a certain cupboard whilst he was playing, but that it was unexpectedly moved to a different cupboard in his absence. The child therefore knows where the chocolate *really* is, but is asked where Maxi will *look* for the chocolate. Wimmer and Perner found that 3-year-olds tend to fail this task, saying that Maxi will look where the chocolate really is, whereas from 4 years upwards, children realise that Maxi's search will be governed by his false belief. This result has been replicated many times (e.g. Baron-Cohen, Leslie, & Frith, 1985; Leekam & Perner, 1991), even when real people rather than dolls are used as the protagonists (Leslie & Frith, 1988), or the child's mother administers the task (Shaw, 1989).

The majority of 4-year-olds also understand how they have gained the knowledge required to pass false belief tasks. This development in understanding the sources of knowledge was demonstrated by Hogrefe, Wimmer, and Perner (1986) in what has become known as the "Smarties task". Hogrefe et al. found that, when asked what was inside a tube of Smarties, 3- and 4-year-olds would answer (unsurprisingly) that the tube contained Smarties. They were then shown that the tube really contained a pencil, and were asked what a class mate would say was in the tube before it had been opened. Four-year-olds tend to pass this task, realising that the other child will be ignorant of the fact that the tube contains a pencil, but 3-year-olds tend to say that the other child will know that there is a pencil in the tube. Gopnik and Astington (1988) showed that children of this age have equal difficulties in attributing the false belief to *themselves* when asked what *they thought* was in the tube before it was opened. Wimmer and Hartl (1991) showed that some 3-year-olds will deny their original answer in the Smarties task even if the experimenter overtly reminds them of what they first said. Moreover, it appears that 3-year-olds' resistance to recognising *their own* initial mistake is not due to embarrassment at getting the answer wrong, since Wimmer and Hartl reported that they found it equally difficult to ascribe the initial mistake to a puppet.

This period also sees important developments in the understanding of the aspectuality of knowledge, since by the age of 4, children understand how different types of informational access relate to different aspects of reality (O'Neill, Astington, & Flavell, 1992; Taylor, Cartwright, & Bowden, 1991). For example, children realise that people need sufficient perceptual information in order to identify a picture, and that people can see different things from different positions. Despite Piaget's claim that perspective-taking abilities do not develop until the end of the pre-operational period (Piaget & Inhelder, 1956), a number of studies have shown that much younger children can show an understanding of another person's orientation to an aspect of physical reality (e.g. Lempers, Flavell, & Flavell, 1977; Light & Nix, 1983). In addition, 4-year-olds are able to understand how pictures and photographs can be used to represent such aspects of reality (Perner & Leekam, 1990; Zaitchik, 1990), something which pre-operational children find very difficult using the "three mountains" paradigm (Piaget & Inhelder, 1956). Preoperational children can even understand how different people will interpret photographs in different ways, realising that, although a picture looks the right way up to one person, it may look upside-down to someone else (Flavell, Everett, Croft, & Flavell, 1981).

THE FALSE BELIEF TASK AS AN INDEX OF MENTALISING ABILITIES

Many researchers (e.g. Moore & Frye, 1991; Olson, Astington, & Harris, 1988; Perner, 1991) have drawn the conclusion that these various achievements are related, but there is considerable disagreement about how these changes come about. The literature on the mechanisms and processes involved in acquiring a "theory of mind" (Premack & Woodruff, 1978) is vast, and I do not intend to outline all of the possible theories here. However, it is worthwhile to discuss two of the major theories of the child's acquisition of an understanding of mind: the "theory" theory (e.g. Gopnik & Wellman, 1992; Perner, 1991) and "simulation" theory (Harris, 1991; Johnson, 1988).

According to the former theory, acquiring an understanding of mind involves qualitative changes in one's representational system, each step building upon the last in a Piagetian fashion. The process begins at around age 2, but at this early stage children's mental lives consist only of desires and perceptions, and they are unable to understand beliefs. Theory theorists therefore maintain that the child's early understanding of mind is non-representational. By 3 years, children have moved into a transitional stage, where they are able to understand representational states like belief, but this understanding is based on direct causal links between the world and people's beliefs about it. Consequently, 3-year-olds cannot understand beliefs which are misrepresentations of reality, and therefore fail false belief tasks. Finally, the child reorganises his or her theory to account for the fact that what people believe or think is governed by their *representations* of reality, not by reality itself. In this transition from one understanding of mind to the next, "[c]hildren should ignore certain kinds of counter-evidence initially, then account for them by auxiliary hypotheses, then use the new theoretical idea in limited contexts, and only finally reorganize their knowledge so that new theoretical entities play a central role" (Gopnik & Wellman, 1992, p.149). According to this view, the understanding of mind therefore involves the acquisition of a *theory* of mind.

In contrast, proponents of the simulation theory, such as Harris (1991), maintain that the child does not have to acquire a theory in order to be able to understand what another person believes or desires—all that is required is experience of a wide enough range of situational possibilities for a child to be able to imagine what he or she would do in another person's position. Harris detailed three steps in the attainment of an understanding of other minds: (1) the capacity for pretence; (2) reasoning with pretend premises; and (3) altering "default settings". The first of these steps is self-explanatory, and as I discussed in previous chapters, children are capable of pretence by 18 months of age. Secondly, children must become skilled in reasoning with pretend premises, which they achieve by recognising that pretence can be based on something which is true in reality or which is really false. For example, the most famous case of children pretending at something which is true *in reality*, is documented by Vygotsky (1933) in his account of two sisters "pretending" to be sisters. They achieved this by changing their everyday mode of sisterly behaviour into an overt and idealised mode, which outwardly displayed their sisterhood. Finally, children may alter their current mental state or that of the world—the so-called default settings. Altering the default settings involves suspending one's own perspective and recognising that another's perspective is equally valid. To use an example from Study Three, the child could dispense with his or her own pretence that the blue napkin was a blanket, and alter the default settings to accommodate the experimenter's perspective of the napkin being a swimming pool for the doll. The argument is that 2-year-olds are able to alter default settings at this level since they do not have to represent the other person's *beliefs*; they simply have to see that the other person has a different view on some aspect of reality. However, in the classic unexpected transfer task, children not only require an understanding of belief, but need to be cognisant of the fact that action is governed by belief, since in order to pass this task children must predict the protagonist's *behaviour*. Harris therefore argued that there is no reason why behaviour which betrays an understanding of other minds should be based on a theory: "children make predictions about other people's actions, thoughts and emotions by running a simulation [which] calls for a working model of the other person but not a theory" (1991, p.299).

Somewhat unsurprisingly, the debate centring on the differential merits of the theory theory and simulation theory has become involved, and is not strictly relevant to the present discussion. Nevertheless, it is necessary to deal with one piece of evidence which has been cited in support of the theory theory, since a related experiment on false belief and emotion was one of the tasks which was performed in Study Five. Wellman (1990) asserted that understanding other minds is theory-based since children often invoke a character's beliefs and desires to explain behaviour. When asked why a character is looking under the piano for her cat, 3- and 4-year-olds will explain this behaviour by saying that the character wants her cat or thinks that it is under the piano (Bartsch & Wellman, 1989; Wellman & Banerjee, 1991). Now consider a study by Harris, Johnson, Hutton, Andrews, and Cooke (1989), which investigated the relationship between false belief and emotion. In this task, a toy animal gets a nasty surprise when a container of its favourite drink turns out to contain a drink which it does not like, e.g. a Coke can filled with milk. Children were asked to say whether the animal felt happy or sad *before* it had drunk anything from the Coke can. This task is more complicated than the standard unexpected transfer task, since it involves the additional component of having to predict the appropriate emotional response. Consequently, the majority of 4-year-olds have difficulty in answering the test question correctly, and say that the animal will feel sad, because there is no Coke in the can. Harris argued that in order to account for children's understanding of other minds, any explanation must account not just for situations which induce correct causal explanations (as reported by Wellman and colleagues above), but for children's responses in the false belief and emotion task, where empathy with a character's feelings and desires appears to lead to incorrect causal explanations.

Harris argued that the anomaly in these findings causes problems for the theory theory, but can be explained by invoking simulation theory's default settings. Older children not only imagine what it would be like to be faced with the can of Coke which really contains milk (which 4-year-olds can imagine), but are able to alter the default settings further to take into account how the character would feel when faced with the situation *as it first appears*; in other words, that there is Coke in the Coke can. Since 4-year-olds have already acquired a theory of mind which can cope with false belief, it is difficult for the theory theorists to explain why children of this age have problems with the false belief and emotion task, except in terms of a general increase in processing demands.

The simulation theory has a further advantage over the theory theory. Namely, since the simulation explanation does not require children to be mini-scientists who construct theories on the basis of their observations, there is no need to postulate mechanisms to account for how the observations are elevated into theories. Instead Harris suggested that children simply attend to others' behaviour and note any regularities which occur. Understanding what another person may believe, do or desire in a certain situation is therefore "based on an assumed analogy between self and other" (1991, p.301).

For present purposes, what is interesting about simulation theory is its common ground with the ideas of other researchers who have stressed the importance of intersubjective experience, rather than a theory of mind, in understanding other people's minds. Trevarthen (1977) has argued that infants are *actively* involved in experiencing other people's minds in the first year of life, since they engage in "the mutual adjustments of conscious voluntary agents (subjects) to one another's mental states" (p.5). Hobson (1993) has also stressed the importance of interaction in achieving an understanding of other minds, arguing that "a conceptual grasp of the nature of "minds" ... is acquired through an individual's experience of affectively patterned, inter-subjectively co-ordinated relations *with* other people" (Hobson, 1993, pp.4-5, original emphasis). In other words, it is direct *experience* of others' mental orientations to the world that determines children's later ability to understand the mental states of others. If this were true, one might expect to find meaningful individual differences in children's understanding of other minds.

INDIVIDUAL DIFFERENCES IN MENTALISING ABILITIES

If direct experience of other people's perspectives on and beliefs about the world is instrumental in bringing about an understanding of other minds, then one should predict that individuals who have more opportunities for gleaning such experiences will show precocity in their mentalising abilities. The most obvious arena in which young children experience other minds is the family, and several researchers have investigated whether familial differences affect children's understanding of other minds. Perner, Ruffman, and Leekam (1994) reported that children who had more siblings performed better on mentalising tasks. These results have been replicated by Jenkins and Astington (1996), who found that family size was still a predictor of mentalising abilities when age and linguistic ability were accounted for, and that siblings could actually mitigate the effects of lower language competence in false belief understanding. Lewis, Freeman, Kyriakidou, Maridaki-Kassotaki, and Berridge (1996) have recently shown that it is not just the nuclear family which is important in this respect. In their study of Greek and Cypriot children, Lewis et al. found that children who had frequent contact with members of their extended families performed better on a battery of false belief tasks.

One reason why family size might be related to children's understanding of other minds is that larger families will see more expression of different points of view, particularly in the context of disputes. Such occurrences tend to give these children greater exposure to mental state language, since it is likely that these disputes will be resolved with reference to the mental states of those involved. This suggestion is supported by a number of studies conducted by Dunn and colleagues. For example, Dunn, Brown, Slomkowski, Tesla, and Youngblade (1991) found that children's ability at 40 months to explain a puppet's behaviour in terms of its false belief was related to their mothers' attempts to control the behaviour of older siblings and encourage cooperative interaction with the sibling when these children were 33 months. Dunn et al. also reported a relationship between false belief understanding and children's participation in family conversations about feelings and causality seven months earlier.

Maternal sensitivity and responsiveness would appear to be important factors in this process. Only mothers who are concerned about resolving disputes fairly and using them to teach their children basic principles might be expected to engage in this type of causal talk and control of older siblings. Given the established link between maternal sensitivity and security of attachment, we have a clear reason for expecting security-related differences in mentalising abilities.

SECURITY OF ATTACHMENT AND MENTALISING ABILITIES

In addition to the family-based effects discussed above, there are a number of reasons to suggest that security of attachment and children's experiences of the mental states of others might be related: (1) securely attached children appear to demonstrate referential tendencies in acquiring language (Study Two); (2) securely attached children are better at acting upon the perspective of another within the context of pretend play (Study Three); (3) mothers of securely attached children present them with information and instructions which are comprehensible and pitched within the ZPD (Study Four); and (4) there is some evidence that the speech of mothers who have securely attached children contains more mental state terms (Fonagy, Steele, Steele, Higgitt, & Target, 1994).

To take the first of these reasons, the results of Study Two showed that securely attached children's early vocabularies contained a high proportion of common nouns and a lack of frozen phrases (such as "clever girl" or "here it is"). Insecurely attached children's early language showed the opposite pattern. I argued that, given these children's inexperience in language production, the referential aspects of language acquisition typical of the secure group gave them more scope to become involved in linguistic exchanges and initiate "conversations" with others. This was possible because referential speech is easier to understand (e.g. Nelson, 1981), and linguistically naive children are more capable of talking about objects than using language interpersonally (see Chapter Four). The linguistic exchanges of the securely attached children are therefore more likely to be truly dialogic, and since they have the capacity to talk about objects, these object-centred exchanges will provide the child with experience of other perspectives on the world from a very early age (Hobson, 1989; Werner & Kaplan, 1963). For example, the child may label the object as a ball, the mother may label it as yellow, and so on.

The second reason for expecting security-based differences in mentalising abilities relates to the findings of Study Three, which showed differences between securely and insecurely attached children in their ability to incorporate another's suggestion into a sequence of symbolic play. If securely attached children are better able to recognise and act upon the perspectives of others in a play scenario, it may well be that these children will be better at representing such perspectival differences at the level of belief. In addition, at the end of Chapter Six, I argued that the behaviour of the mothers in the secure group on the tutoring task (e.g. constantly using feedback from the child's performance to alter the specificity of subsequent instructions, interacting within the ZPD, etc.) could be construed as evidence for the greater proclivity of these mothers to treat their children as mental agents.

The fourth reason for expecting security-based differences in mentalising abilities relates to the findings of Fonagy et al. (1994). They found that mothers of securely attached children scored more highly on a "reflective self scale" (Fonagy, Steele, Moran, Steele, & Higgitt, 1991), indicating that these mothers are more likely to invoke mental states in describing the behaviour of others. One might therefore expect that securely attached children will have had greater experience of adults' use of mental state terms to describe and explain individuals' behaviour.

In my view, the most interesting interpretation of this suggestion is that mothers in the secure group consider their children to be sufficiently sophisticated to understand the mental lives of others—people's beliefs, desires, intentions, and so on—and this may account for their greater sensitivity and responsiveness (e.g. Ainsworth, Bell, & Stayton, 1971). However, I should caution that Fonagy et al. only investigated differences in mothers' use of mental state terms within the context of the Adult Attachment Interview (George, Kaplan, & Main, 1985). Although it seems reasonable to assume that mothers' answers during this interview reflect their normal speaking patterns, this has not yet been established empirically.

To date, the evidence for the predicted link between security of attachment and mentalising abilities has been somewhat sparse. In a review of the literature on the relationship between metacognitive functioning and security of attachment, Main (1991) proposed that children's early experiences with their caregivers are important for their subsequent metacognitive knowledge and monitoring of attachment experiences. Main argued that "experiences with the parents may not only alter the *contents* of the young child's mind, but may alter *her ability to operate upon those contents*" (p.129, original emphasis). This argument was based on the premise that securely attached children will be better able to attend to and reassess reality, since they are secure in the knowledge that the caregiver is available for support. In contrast, insecurely attached children will be less able to turn their full attention to the environment, since they have to monitor the caregiver's physical whereabouts and psychological accessibility. Main reported the results of various pilot studies to support her argument. For example, securely attached 6-year-olds spontaneously acknowledged that different people could feel different emotions in the same situation, gave reflective answers when questioned about their thoughts, and realised that other people could not know what they were thinking.

More recently, Fonagy, Redfern, and Charman (1997) assessed a group of 3- to 6-year-olds on the Separation Anxiety Test (Klagsbrun & Bowlby, 1976) and a version of Harris et al.'s (1989) false belief and emotion task. They found that children who were classified as secure in their representations of attachment were more likely to pass the false belief and emotion task. These studies thus show a *concurrent* relationship between security of attachment and the understanding of other minds, but they did not address the question of whether *infantile* security of attachment is a predictor of mentalising abilities in early childhood. This was the aim of Study Five.

Study Five describes a series of experiments performed by Fernyhough (1994) on the groups of securely and insecurely attached children who participated in the studies reported in the earlier chapters. Two hypotheses were tested in this study. Firstly, it was predicted that, at four years of age, securely attached children will be more likely than their insecure peers to pass a version of the standard "unexpected transfer" task (Wimmer & Perner, 1983). Secondly, it was predicted that the secure group's superior performance will carry over to tasks involving a more complex understanding of other minds, such as the relationship between belief and emotion, administered at five years. The possibility that any such differences might be due to general differences in cognitive ability was addressed by assessing the children on standardised ability scales.

STUDY FIVE[1]

Subjects were 33 (13 girls, 20 boys) of the original children who had taken part in the four studies reported in the previous chapters. Twenty-five of these subjects (11 girls, 14 boys) were assessed at age 4 (range 47 to 50 months) on a version of the unexpected transfer task (described below). The follow-up at 5 years (range 60 to 62 months) was carried out with all 33 subjects. Of the 33 subjects, 19 were classified as securely attached, 6 were insecure-avoidant, 4 were insecure-resistant and 4 were insecure-disorganised. With respect to SES, 13 (8 secure and 5 insecure) children were classified as status 1, and 20 (11 secure and 9 insecure) children were status 2.

AGE 4 ASSESSMENT

The unexpected transfer task (Wimmer and Perner, 1983)

Seated at a table with the experimenter, children were introduced to a soft toy called Charlie the Crocodile, and asked to guess what his favourite food was. After guessing, subjects were told that Charlie's favourite food was chocolate. A chocolate was placed in one of two small cardboard boxes, one red and the other white. Subjects were told that Charlie was hiding his chocolate to keep it safe while he went for a swim. Charlie was then removed from the table, and the experimenter told the child that they were going to play a trick on Charlie. The experimenter took the chocolate out of the box in which it had been hidden and placed it in the other box, closing both lids. Subjects were told that Charlie was about to return from his swim, and that he would be wanting his chocolate. The following questions were then asked:

Where was the chocolate in the beginning?
Where is the chocolate now?
Does Charlie know where the chocolate is?

If any of these questions were answered incorrectly, the story was briefly repeated and the three questions asked again. If the child failed to answer correctly the second time, he or she was excluded from the analysis. When correct answers had been given on each of the three questions, the test question was presented: Where does Charlie think the chocolate is?[2]

AGE 5 ASSESSMENT

The children were followed-up a year later with two further tests involving an understanding of other minds, and their general cognitive ability was assessed at this age, using the British Picture Vocabulary Scale (Dunn, Dunn, Whetton, & Pintilie, 1982). The children were tested in two sessions separated by at least a week. In the first session, the British Picture Vocabulary Scale (BPVS) was administered, followed by the "picture identification task" (Taylor, Cartwright, & Bowden, 1991). The "false belief and emotion task" (Harris et al., 1989) was given in the second session.

The picture identification task
This task was derived from that of Taylor et al. (1991). Children were first introduced to a soft toy called Freddy the Frog and the box in which he lived. The box was said to be special because, when Freddy was inside, he was unable to see anything that was going on or hear anything that was being said. Children were then shown a transparency depicting a giraffe and an elephant, and asked what was in the picture. After the subject had answered correctly, the experimenter held the transparency between himself and the child and introduced a cardboard folder between himself and part of the transparency (for example, covering the elephant). The child was then asked to say what the experimenter could see. This was repeated twice, finishing with the folder obscuring both the elephant and the giraffe. No child had any difficulty in understanding the experimenter's perspective in this way.

Subjects were asked if they remembered what was special about Freddy's box, and reminded if they had forgotten. They were then told that they were going to see some pictures. Six pictures were used, representing three kinds of view. For two of the pictures (a dog and a man) the part visible was sufficient to allow the object in the picture to be identified (i.e. the head). In the second pair of pictures (a bed and a ship), part of the object was visible, but insufficient to allow identification. In the final pair of pictures (a pig and a boot), the hole was cut so that no part of the picture was visible.

The order of presentation of the pictures was randomised. The first closed folder was shown to the subject, who was asked what he or she thought was in the picture. Once the child had answered, the experimenter opened the folder to show what was actually in the picture. He then closed the folder, took Freddy the Frog out of his box and placed him in front of the closed folder. The child was asked whether Freddy knew what was in the picture. The number of "no" responses to the "nondescript" views was taken as a measure of the child's understanding of the relation between informational access and picture interpretation. Any children who demonstrated a negative or positive response bias were excluded from the analysis.

The false belief and emotion task

The final task was derived from Harris et al.'s (1989) study of young children's understanding of the causal role of beliefs in determining emotional responses. In order to be successful on this task, subjects were required to understand not only a character's current belief, but also to integrate this information with previous knowledge about the character's preferences and desires in order to predict an emotional response. In the present version of the task, children were introduced to four toy animals. It was explained that Charlie the Crocodile was going to play a trick on each of the animals in turn. For each animal, a story was told about the animal's favourite food. For example, subjects were told, "Freddy the Frog wants a snack, but he only likes one kind of snack, and that's Twiglets (pointing to a box of Twiglets). He doesn't like crisps (pointing to a box of crisps); he only likes Twiglets." Freddy the Frog was removed from the table, and Charlie the Crocodile was then seen to remove the Twiglets from their box and replace them with crisps. All containers were opaque, so that the contents were not visible. The child was then asked: (a) what Freddy's preference was; and (b) what was actually in the box now. If either of these questions was answered incorrectly, the scenario was briefly redescribed. Freddy was then returned to the table, at which point the following test questions were asked:

1. How does Freddy feel when he is first given the box? Does he feel happy or does he feel sad?
2. How does Freddy feel when he looks inside the box and finds there are crisps instead of Twiglets? Does he feel happy or does he feel sad?

The measure of subjects' understanding of the link between false belief and emotion was the number of correct answers to question 1 (maximum score = 4). In the few cases where children gave incorrect responses to question 2, it was usually the result of a general bias towards positive or negative answers. These children were excluded from the analysis. In order to control for biases due to the characters being toys rather than people, children were asked to justify their answers to questions 1 and 2. If these justifications suggested that the child had forgotten the animal's preference or the nature of the trick, the salient information was repeated and the questions reiterated. Thus, the experimenter was able to ensure that incorrect answers on question 2 were due to a specific problem in integrating information about the animal's beliefs and desires, rather than to memory failure or response bias[3].

RESULTS

The results for the assessments made at 4 years of age showed that securely attached children were more likely to pass the standard unexpected transfer task than their insecurely attached peers: 83% of the secure group answered correctly, compared with 33% of the insecure group. This difference was significant at the 0.025 level. Considering the children from the three insecure attachment groups who passed the control questions, 2 out of 5 insecure-avoidant children passed the unexpected transfer task, compared with one of the 3 insecure-disorganised children; only one insecure-resistant child passed the control questions, and this child went on to fail the test question.

On the picture identification task, 11 out of 13 children in the secure group gave the maximum two correct attributions on the nondescript views, compared with 5 out of 10 in the insecure group. This difference was significant at the 0.05 level. The difference between the secure and insecure groups in the mean number of correct attributions (1.77 for the secure group; 1.10 for the insecure group) approached significance (p = 0.07). The mean number of correct attributions for the three insecure attachment groups were as follows: insecure-avoidant = 1.00; insecure-resistant = 1.00; insecure-disorganised = 1.33. On the false belief and emotion task, the mean number of correct answers to Question 1 (see p.122) was 2.25 for the secure group and 1.62 for the insecure group, which represented a non-significant trend in the predicted direction. For the three insecure attachment groups, the mean number of correct answers to Question 1 were: 2.22 for the insecure-avoidant group, 0.83 for the insecure-resistant group and 1.50 for the insecure-disorganised group.

In addition, there were no differences between the secure and insecure groups on the BPVS[4]. Taking the mean standardised BPVS score as 100, the mean for the secure group was 113.30, compared with 110.50 for the insecure group. The mean scores for the three insecure groups were as follows: insecure-avoidant group = 114; insecure-resistant group = 99; insecure-disorganised group = 118.25.

When the data were analysed according to whether the subject solved the unexpected transfer task at age 4, scores on the false belief and emotion task were significantly higher for the successful group than for the unsuccessful group, and there was a non-significant trend in the same direction for the picture identification task. The security-based differences on any of these tasks could not be explained with respect to the children's SES.

The study outlined above found that: (1) 4-year-olds who were securely attached in infancy were more likely than their insecurely-attached peers to pass a version of the standard unexpected transfer task (Wimmer & Perner, 1983); when assessed at age 5, (2) securely attached children were better able to understand another character's knowledge of a picture; and (3) there was a non-significant trend for children in the secure group to outperform their insecurely attached counterparts on a task requiring an understanding of how emotions are determined by belief. In terms of the proportions of children passing these tasks, the results of Study Five were in line with those of previous researchers (Harris et al., 1989; Taylor et al., 1991; Wimmer & Perner, 1983). The finding of no difference between the secure and insecure groups in their general level of cognitive ability is also in line with previous studies (see van IJzendoorn et al., 1995). When the data were classified according to whether the subject had passed the unexpected transfer task at age 4, the successful children performed better on the more complex mentalising tasks at age 5. Finally, although the numbers of children in the three insecure attachment groups were too small for statistical analysis, the group means on the false belief and emotion task are of interest. The insecure-resistant group performed worse than their counterparts in the avoidant and disorganised groups on this task. It is possible that the inconsistent patterns of caregiving observed in the mothers of resistant children (Isabella, 1993; Isabella & Belsky, 1991) may go some way to explain their poorer performance on a task which requires an understanding of the relationship between emotions and beliefs. This is an interesting finding, worthy of future research with a larger sample of children.

What features of the secure attachment relationship might account for these children's apparent advantage on tasks designed to assess mentalising abilities? In the Introduction to this chapter, I set out a number of possible reasons why such differences might be expected (pp.117–119). For example, I suggested that early linguistic acquisitional style might be an important factor in this respect. To recap, it was noted in Chapter Four that securely attached children's tendency to acquire a high proportion of common nouns in their early vocabularies might give them greater control and flexibility within linguistic exchanges. In addition, I described how having conversations about objects which are physically present will mean that these children will be exposed to other people's orientations to reality: the child labels the object as "dolly", the mother labels the same object as "pretty", and so on. Study Two's finding that secure group mothers were unlikely to report "vocal but meaningless" utterances, implying that they are more willing to treat their children's utterances as intentional, may also help us to understand these security-related differences in mentalising abilities.

The second reason for predicting such differences stemmed from the results of Study Three, which found that securely attached children were better able to respond to the different perspective of an experimenter within a symbolic play situation. I argued that securely attached children's greater ability to adopt the perspective of the other might later manifest itself in more advanced mentalising performance. The conjecture that this advantage might stem from such children's experience of more sensitive and responsive dyadic interaction was supported by the findings of Study Four, which showed that mothers of securely attached children were more sensitive tutors, and tended to give over responsibility for the task to their children. Finally, I suggested that secure-group mothers' greater tendency to use mentalistic terms in their speech might be a further reason for expecting security-related differences in mentalising abilities.

Despite the lack of a relationship between security of attachment and general cognitive ability, it is conceivable that there is some *specific* cognitive ability underlying performance on tasks which require an understanding of other minds. For example, securely attached children may be born with more highly developed innate mentalising capacities (of the sort specified, for example, in Baron-Cohen, 1995), which give them an early advantage in understanding other minds. But an account of these findings in terms of differences in an innately-specified "metarepresentational capacity" (e.g. Leslie & Frith, 1990) seems to be unsatisfactory, since it is difficult to see why securely attached children should be more well-endowed with such a capacity. Of course, it could be that securely attached infants' superior innate capacities themselves *cause* their differential treatment by caregivers and family members, and thus determine the quality of the emerging attachment relationship. However, this seems unlikely for a number of reasons.

First, mothers would have to show differential sensitivity to very early occurring mentalising capacities long before, on the modularist account, these capacities are said to emerge. Second, a view of the secure attachment relationship as being caused by an innate advantage in mentalising would not fit well with the finding of differences in security of attachment with caregivers within the same family (e.g. Belsky & Rovine, 1987; Lamb et al., 1982; Main & Weston, 1982). A more satisfactory account of the observed differences between the mentalising abilities of the secure and insecure groups would see these effects as resulting from, rather than causing, the experience of a secure attachment relationship. On such a view, the only innate characteristic which would seem fundamental to the acquisition of mentalising abilities would be the infant's biologically specified socioaffective responsivity, about which I will have more to say in the final chapter.

The fact that a child can have a secure attachment to one caregiver and an insecure attachment to another does, however, raise an interesting question with respect to issues of quality and quantity of sensitive caregiving. For example, is a single secure attachment sufficient to confer these advantages on the child's ability to understand other minds? Alternatively, if children have secure attachments to several caregivers, do these have an additive effect on the child's mentalising abilities? Finally, could it be that one insecure attachment leaches away the advantages conveyed by a secure attachment with another caregiver? Unfortunately, since the studies reported here are based only on the child's attachment to mother, these questions cannot yet be answered. This shortcoming highlights the need to view the correlates and consequences of attachment within the context of the whole family system. However, my data are representative of these children's security of attachment to the *primary* caregiver, and such distinctions between primary and secondary caregivers should be made explicit in future research. It may be that, regardless of attachments to secondary caregivers, if the child is securely attached to the primary caregiver, then his or her profile will be that of a securely attached child. For example, Main, Kaplan, and Cassidy (1985) found that the child's security of attachment to mother in infancy continued to be a strong predictor of various aspects of the child's behaviour at age 6. In contrast, children's early security of attachment to father showed little relation to their functioning in childhood. Of course, identifying the primary caregiver may prove to be increasingly difficult, given changes in caregiving practices. If children have been placed in daycare from an early age, and have been continually looked after by a particular carer, it may be that this person is the child's primary attachment figure. Moreover, with changes in traditional bread-winning roles, especially in lower SES groups, it may be that many more fathers are taking on child-rearing responsibilities, thus becoming primary attachment figures.

There is still much to be done in setting out precisely which factors are important in determining the cognitive consequences of the secure attachment relationship. In addition, further work is needed to establish whether these cognitive effects of security of attachment are direct, or whether they are mediated by, for example, greater symbolic or linguistic ability. Such questions will be my focus of attention in the last chapter. In the meantime, it is worth drawing out one point which seems especially pertinent to the results of Study Five, and which might help us to make sense of the growing literature on social influences on mentalising abilities. Namely, that a mother's *mind-mindedness*—her recognition of her child as a mental agent, and her proclivity to employ mental state terms in her speech—would appear to play an important role in the child's developing understanding of other minds.

Although a full exploration of this body of research lies beyond the scope of this chapter (see Fernyhough, 1997), it is worth mentioning at least three possibilities, which may not be mutually exclusive, for how maternal mind-mindedness may affect children's developing mentalising abilities. First, mothers' tendency to treat their children as mental agents may scaffold children's acquisition of their culture's folk "theory of mind" (Astington, 1996; Lewis et al., 1996) through the mother's ability accurately to identify her child's zone of proximal development. Second, such interaction may expose the child to mental state language, thus scaffolding the acquisition of mental concepts such as belief and desire, which will subsequently play a role in a fully conceptual theory of mind. Third, sensitive reciprocal interaction of this sort will allow the effective internalisation of dialogic exchanges, which will in turn underpin children's ability to accommodate multiple perspectives on reality (Fernyhough, 1996). It goes without saying that teasing apart these possibilities will require a great deal of empirical and theoretical work. However, it would seem that the concept of mind-mindedness captures an important aspect of the secure attachment relationship, with all its implications for the child's developing cognitive abilities.

NOTES

1. I must express my thanks to Chas Fernyhough for allowing me to use his data. These results are published in full as: Meins, E., Fernyhough, C., Russell, J., & Clark-Carter, D. (in press). Security of attachment as a predictor of symbolic and mentalising abilities: A longitudinal study. *Social Development*.

2. It could be argued that asking the test question before the control questions would be a better measure of mentalising ability. However, Lewis (unpublished data) found no effect of reversal in question order on children's performance on the unexpected transfer task.

3. A typical exchange showing such a failure of integration was as follows: Freddy, who prefers crisps, is given a crisps box with Twiglets in it. The child is asked how Freddy will feel when he is first given the box.

Child	Sad.
Experimenter	Why will he feel sad?
Child	Because there's Twiglets inside.
Experimenter	Does he know there are Twiglets inside?
Child	No.

4. These children were also assessed on the matrices component of the British Ability Scales (Elliot, Murray, & Pearson, 1983). No differences were found between the secure and insecure groups on this measure of general cognitive ability.

CHAPTER EIGHT

Implications and applications

As my study of theory progressed it was gradually borne in upon me that the field I had set out to plough so lightheartedly was no less than the one that Freud had started tilling sixty years earlier, and that it contained all those same rocky excrescences and thorny entanglements that he had encountered and grappled with—love and hate, anxiety and defence, attachment and loss. What had deceived me was that my furrows had been started from a corner diametrically opposite to the one at which Freud had entered and through which analysts have always followed. From a new viewpoint a familiar landscape can sometimes look very different. (Bowlby, 1969, p.xi)

I began this book with a discussion of Bowlby's (1958, 1969) theory of infant-mother attachment, noting how his focus on separation as a psychological trauma was a major force in shaping his theory. I argued that, although psychoanalytical theory was an appropriate starting point for understanding the attachment relationship, an equally valid approach would be to centre on the issues of ego development and expression, and their role in the child's ability to cope with separation from the attachment figure. Such an approach would preserve the psychoanalytic underpinnings of attachment theory, whilst offering a more satisfactory account of the diverse findings relating to infant-mother attachment. In particular, viewing the child's actions upon separation in terms of ego-related processes, rather than psychological trauma, can account for the different *patterns* of attachment observed in the first naturalistic studies of infant-mother interaction (Ainsworth, 1963, 1967; Schaffer & Emerson, 1964).

Another problem with Bowlby's original attachment theory is that it addressed only the making and breaking of attachment relationships: infants were either attached or unattached. It was thus difficult for his theory to encompass the concept of security of attachment posited by Ainsworth (e.g. Ainsworth, Blehar, Waters, & Wall, 1978). Such individual differences pose fewer problems for a theory of attachment based on ego strength and development; indeed, such differences should be expected. In my Vygotskian approach to attachment, I argued that security-based differences may result from securely attached children's greater self-efficacy, nurtured by maternal sensitivity focused in the zone of proximal development (ZPD). The studies in this book set about investigating this claim. Before speculating further on their applications and implications, I should summarise the findings of the five studies I have reported.

A SUMMARY OF THE EMPIRICAL FINDINGS

Study One investigated the relationship between security of attachment and search behaviour on Piagetian object and person permanence tasks between the ages of 11 and 19 months. The results of this study showed that, across the object, mother and stranger permanence tasks, securely attached children achieved a higher level of search. This difference could not be explained by the securely attached children's comparatively greater motivation to regain sight of their mothers, since no décalage effects were found (see pp.52–53). I argued that this was evidence for the securely attached children's greater self-efficacy, since they appeared to be able to use their mental representation of the hidden object or person to initiate search. In contrast, the performance of the insecurely attached children was almost certainly an underestimation of their ability mentally to represent a hidden object, given that several studies have found much younger infants capable of doing so (e.g. Baillargeon, 1987, 1991). Children in the insecure group did not appear to use their cognitive resources optimally in searching for the object or person.

In Study Two, the linguistic acquisitional style of the securely and insecurely attached children was assessed. Differences in the early vocabularies of the two groups were found on three measures of referential language acquisition (Nelson, 1973): securely attached children were faster at acquiring language; their early vocabularies contained a higher proportion of common nouns; and they did not tend to acquire frozen phrases. The acquisitional style of the insecurely attached children showed the opposite pattern, demonstrating aspects of what has been termed expressive linguistic style (Nelson, 1973). Researchers have found a number of interesting differences in children who acquire language via these two routes, although such differences have not previously been considered in relation to security of attachment. For example, referential children are more likely to use objects to initiate social exchanges (Goldfield, 1985, 1986), and their language is easier to understand than that of expressive children (Nelson, 1981). The mothers of referential and expressive children have also been found to differ in their use of language. Referential children's mothers tend to spend more time using language to refer to objects, whilst mothers of expressive children make more references to people (Furrow & Nelson, 1984). Mothers of referential children use more descriptive language, in contrast to the more prescriptive speech of expressive children's mothers (Tomasello & Todd, 1983). I argued that there are strong commonalities between this characterisation of the "referential" dyad and that of the secure mother-child dyad. In particular, I suggested that the apparent "referential" flavour of securely attached children's acquisitional style is consistent with their greater self-efficacy. In addition, acquiring a high proportion of common nouns will give the linguistically inexperienced child more control in social exchanges, by allowing him or her to choose a topic of conversation by using an object word. This suggestion is supported by the results of Bretherton et al.'s (1979) study on attachment and communication, which found that the best predictor of security of attachment at 12 months was children's declarative pointing one month earlier.

The securely attached child's use of the mother as a secure base for exploring the world, punctuating these explorations with physical or visual references to her, may thus set up a process of interaction whereby objects and their surroundings become important as factors directing communicative exchanges. As children start to speak, past experience of such exchanges will be reflected in the type of words they acquire. In addition, the greater clarity of referential children's speech suggests that they will be able to communicate with people other than their caregivers. Finally, I added a note of caution concerning a potential confound relating to the possibility that mothers of securely attached children were more motivated to monitor their children's vocabularies, and recognise that they were using certain vocalisations to convey specific meanings. Such caution seems warranted, given the secure group mothers' tendency not to report "vocal but meaningless" utterances (Study Two). This potential confound may in turn be a function of mothers' proclivity to attribute mental states to their children. I return to these possible differences in "mind-mindedness" (see pp.108–109 and 127) later in this chapter.

Study Three investigated whether the observed differences in language between the secure and insecure groups carried over to their capacity for symbolism in play. Previous work by Belsky, Garduque and Hrncir (1984) had reported that securely attached 12- to 18-month-olds were more likely than their insecurely attached peers spontaneously to play at a level near to their maximum competence for pretence. These securely attached children, unlike those in the insecure group, did not benefit to any great extent from being told or shown how to pretend by an experimenter. Slade (1987b), however, found that the play of securely attached 20- to 28-month-olds improved with maternal involvement. The results of Study Three were consistent with those of Slade, and extended her findings to address the role of *non*-maternal involvement in children's play. Of the 2½-year-olds who took part in Study Three, the securely attached children benefited more from the experimenter's instructions than those who were insecurely attached. The apparent discrepancy between the results of Belsky et al. and those of Study Three was explained with reference to the differing ages of the subjects and the different play materials and procedures used in the two studies. Belsky et al. used toys which were miniatures of adult objects, and modelled the desired sequence of pretence, whereas most of the play materials in Study Three were junk objects with no obvious function, and the pretend sequences were encouraged in a more open-ended fashion, without any modelling.

Study Three provided two further interesting findings: (1) there was no difference in the sophistication of pretend play between the secure and insecure groups *before* the experimenter intervened; and (2) insecurely attached children were more likely to ignore the experimenter's suggestion and continue with the sequence of pretence which they had devised. Securely attached children appeared to demonstrate their superiority after intervention in being able to collaborate with the experimenter in order to alter and enrich their sequences of pretence. This led to the conclusion that there may be differences between the secure and insecure groups in their social flexibility, possibly related to their earlier experiences of responsive interpersonal interaction.

Such an interpretation would be in line with Vygotsky's (e.g. 1934/1986) views on the importance of interpersonal exchange in the child's mental development, while also highlighting the importance of the *quality* of the ensuing exchanges. I argued that what distinguishes the mothers of securely attached children from their counterparts in the insecure group is their ability to set up interactions which are pitched at the most appropriate and stimulating level for their children. In order to do so, these mothers must be capable of recognising not only their children's actual level of ability, but also their *potential*, and thus "take stock of processes that are now in the state of coming into being, that are only ripening or developing" (Vygotsky, 1956, pp.447-8). In other words, the mothers in the secure group seemed better able to interact with their children within the ZPD.

This claim was supported by the results of Study Four, which investigated mothers' abilities to tutor their children on a collaborative box construction task. The mothers of securely attached children "scaffolded" (Wood, Bruner, & Ross, 1976) their children's performance by giving them positive rather than negative feedback, intervening with physical help only when the children requested it, and using feedback from their children's performance to alter the specificity of their subsequent comments. Although there was no relationship between SES and security of attachment for the children who participated in Study Four, there was a suspicion that the differences between the secure and insecure groups in the use of positive and negative feedback may have been related to SES, since significant differences were found between the higher and lower SES groups on these measures. The other differences in tutoring strategy were, however, unrelated to SES, and seemed to be a specific function of the security of the attachment relationship.

Mothers of securely attached children thus appear more adept at interacting with them within the ZPD, encouraging them to do things for themselves when they are able, and giving over to them some degree of responsibility for the task. I went on to suggest that one way of explaining this difference is in terms of mothers' mind-mindedness, that is, their proclivity to construe their children as mental agents. This led to the prediction that securely attached children may be better at understanding different perspectives at the level of belief.

Study Five tested this prediction using a series of tasks which required an understanding of other minds. At 4 years, securely attached children were found to be more likely than their insecurely attached peers to pass a version of the unexpected transfer task (Wimmer & Perner, 1983). At age 5, securely attached children performed better on tasks which required either an understanding of someone else's knowledge of a picture, or of how emotions are determined by beliefs. Study Five was important for another reason, in that it assessed these children's general cognitive ability using the British Picture Vocabulary Scale (Dunn et al., 1982). No differences were found between the secure and insecure groups, which is in line with the findings of previous researchers in this area (see van IJzendoorn et al., 1995).

A VYGOTSKIAN APPROACH TO ATTACHMENT

The findings of the five studies described in the previous chapters[1] appear to be independent of children's cognitive ability and SES. The observed effects cannot therefore be reduced to underlying differences at a general cognitive or social level; rather, they seem to be a specific function of security of attachment. My task in this chapter is to suggest which facets of the infant-mother relationship may be instrumental in bringing about the observed differences. I have suggested that a Vygotskian approach to attachment may be a useful framework within which to understand the relationship between the social construct of attachment and the child's cognitive development. The first aim of this section is thus to outline the major principles on which this approach is based.

Vygotsky's (1978) "general genetic law of cultural development" (see p.13) distinguished psychological functioning *between* individuals (the interpsychological plane) from psychological functioning *within* the individual (the intrapsychological plane). The latter is formed through a process of internalisation of interactions which have occurred between the child and others on the interpsychological plane. According to Vygotsky, young infants will only be able to function on the interpsychological plane, because the internalisation process will not be well developed. It is through internalising interactions on the interpsychological plane that the child develops the *higher mental functions*, such as verbal thought. The higher mental functions arise from social interaction, are accessible to consciousness and are semiotically mediated by culturally-derived systems of language and gesture.

This process of internalisation has been observed during collaborative tasks between mothers and children. Wertsch and Stone (1985) discussed how children gradually become able to internalise the dialogic exchanges between themselves and their caregivers, and thus increasingly rely on their own thought processes, rather than on instruction from the caregiver, to complete a task. For example, Wertsch and Stone described how a 2½-year-old child and her mother approached the task of constructing a jigsaw puzzle of a lorry, using an identical, completed puzzle as a guide. The construction of the section which represented the lorry's cargo provided the most interesting exchanges, since the cargo consisted of differently coloured squares which had to go in specific locations in order for the puzzle to be an exact replica of the model lorry. At first, the child appeared oblivious to the fact that the model puzzle had to be consulted in order for the task to be completed correctly. In these early exchanges, when the child asked where the differently coloured squares had to be placed, the child's mother had to draw her attention to the model puzzle. The child's use of the model puzzle as a guide under these circumstances was thus a feature of the *dyad's* functioning, that is, interaction on the interpsychological plane. However, by the end of the task, the child was able to consult the model puzzle without prompting from her mother, and talked herself through the process of asking where the square went, locating the given square on the model, and then placing it in the corresponding position on her own puzzle. It is thus possible to see how the general genetic law of cultural development is related to the ZPD. Interactions on the interpsychological plane which are pitched within the ZPD will facilitate the process of internalisation, and thus the development of the higher mental functions.

How can this approach aid our understanding of the observed security-related differences? In Chapter One, the similarities between Vygotsky's and Bowlby's approaches to development were discussed. Bowlby's (1969) theory of attachment focused on the dynamics of the *relationship* between the infant and the mother figure, rather than the characteristics of either of the two individuals. Likewise, Vygotsky (1978) placed dyadic interaction at the heart of his theory. Both theories also show an integration of the social and cognitive developmental domains, although Bowlby's theory does little more than recognise that attachment is dependent upon certain cognitive prerequisites, such as object/person permanence. But something important can be gained from a synthesis of Vygotskian and attachment theories, since their strengths are complementary.

As we have seen, Ainsworth's (e.g. 1963, 1967) contribution to attachment research was to demonstrate the existence of individual differences within the infant-mother relationship in the form of secure and insecure patterns of attachment. Attachment theory thus provides an elegant description of individual differences in children's relationships with their caregivers. However, it provides little theoretical basis for explaining why security of attachment is related to the child's cognitive development. We know from the literature that the secure attachment relationship is associated with greater maternal sensitivity and secure base behaviour in the child, but neither of these concepts is particularly useful in explaining the observed differences. For example, how can these factors explain the finding that securely attached children tend to take the referential route into language (Study Two), are better able to adapt their play to incorporate the suggestions of others (Study Three), and are more likely to show an understanding of other minds (Study Five)? Maternal sensitivity and secure base behaviour *per se* cannot offer an explanation of such differences, but these factors do provide a sound starting point for an investigation into the cognitive correlates and consequences of attachment. It is at this point that Vygotsky's ideas on the relationship between social interaction and cognitive development prove enlightening.

It may be that the process of internalisation described by Vygotsky can help us to understand why securely attached children show superior performance on the tasks described here, despite having no advantage over their insecurely attached peers in terms of general cognitive ability. Specifically, the greater sensitivity of mothers whose children are securely attached may allow them to identify more reliably their children's ZPD and to pitch their interactions accordingly. In turn, these interactions will be easier to internalise by the child because they have been presented in a sensitive, contingent manner. The internalisation of such interactions thus does not make securely attached children "brighter" in terms of general cognitive ability, rather, it provides them with guidance on how to approach interactions with the world.

The concept of maternal sensitivity remains, however, somewhat nebulous (see p.37). In order to establish precisely which aspects of maternal sensitivity may be most important with respect to the security-related differences discussed here, I proposed the concept of maternal *mind-mindedness*: the propensity to treat one's infant as an individual with a mind. In the following section, I will discuss the extent to which maternal mind-mindedness and other characteristics of infant-mother interaction provide contexts for the development both of a secure attachment relationship, and of the child's higher mental functions.

CONTEXTS FOR DEVELOPMENT

If interactions between child and caregiver are of such importance for the child's cognitive development, more needs to be known of the processes which facilitate the establishment of a contingent pattern of interaction within the ZPD. Two major questions are of particular interest here. First, which specific interactional contexts will be important in determining the observed attachment-related differences? Second, what are the key features of the maternal behaviours which are associated with a secure attachment relationship? In addressing these questions, I shall argue: (1) that interactions during the early months of life which occur within the ZPD, particularly those centred on objects, are the most important contexts in establishing the secure attachment relationship; (2) that the crucial aspect of maternal behaviour is her mind-mindedness, or propensity to treat her infant as a mental agent; and (3) that the individual characteristics of the child are relatively unimportant.

My task in the remainder of this chapter, therefore, is not merely to revisit the well-documented debate about possible precursors of the secure attachment relationship, such as maternal sensitivity and mothers' working models of attachment (see Chapter Two). Rather, I wish to build on my earlier arguments to consider how these maternal characteristics will determine the quality and content of mothers' early interactions with their infants, and affect the child's subsequent social and cognitive development.

Object-centred interaction

Werner and Kaplan (1963) argued that early object-centred interactions between infant and caregiver help the child to begin to understand about different perspectives on the world. They further maintained that such interactions within the "primordial sharing situation" help the child to understand the basics of symbolic representation. For example, by using different linguistic terms, the same object can be represented in different ways: its shape, its colour, its name, and so on. Hobson (1989, 1993) built on the work of Werner and Kaplan, claiming that the capacity to symbolise is rooted in early social co-referencing situations, where the child has direct experience of the adult's differing perspective on reality. Hobson argued that experiences of this type of exchange may help the infant to develop the ability to abstract linguistic symbol from object. This argument echoes Vygotsky's (1933) ideas on this subject. Vygotsky maintained that children must be able to sever an object's physical appearance from its symbolic meaning before they can begin to understand pretence, because "in play activity thought is separated from objects, and actions arise from ideas rather than from things" (1933, p.546).

Is there any evidence that object-centred interaction is related to individual differences in infant-mother attachment? One could argue that securely attached children will tend to be presented with more opportunities for object-centred dyadic interaction, because of their ability to use the mother as a secure base for exploration. These children tend to punctuate their explorations of the world with references to their mothers, which may take the form of physically returning to her to show her an object, vocalising to attract her attention, or the mother and infant jointly attending to some aspect of the environment. Securely attached children have been shown to spend longer in individual bouts of exploratory behaviour, show greater interest in objects, and spend more time attending to objects (Main, 1973, 1983). In contrast, the behaviour of insecure-avoidant children, although leaning towards exploration, does not involve the mother to the same extent. These infants tend not to use the mother as a reference point for their explorations, and do not involve her in their interactions with objects. Insecure-resistant children will also have reduced opportunities for object-centred interaction because of their over-involvement with the mother. These infants tend not to explore the environment, and will therefore engage in less contact with objects. It is difficult to predict any pattern of object-centred interaction for insecure-disorganised children, but one can imagine that episodes of disorganised functioning will put them at a disadvantage in learning about the world. Similarly, the fact that securely attached children are referential in their language acquisition (see Study Two) may be related to greater opportunities for object-centred interaction. This suggestion is not inconsistent with the findings of Bretherton et al. (1979) on the relationship between declarative pointing and security of attachment (see p.131). Taken together, these findings lead us to predict that the secure dyad may show a preference for interactions which are centred on objects, concentrating less on purely "social" interactions, such as nursery rhymes or peek-a-boo.

These findings may also point towards security-related differences in the ways in which mothers regard their children. For example, securely attached children may show a greater interest in objects because their mothers have tended to interact with them via objects or use objects as "topics of conversation". In the same way, securely attached children may engage in more declarative pointing because their mothers have shown a greater propensity to attribute meaning to their early gestures. There is, however, a question of the direction of causation between infant object-centred action and the caregiver's interpretation of such actions. It may be that the infant becomes interested in objects because *the mother* has preferred to use objects as focal points in their interactions. Alternatively, the mother may have recognised that her infant appears to enjoy looking at and touching objects, and thus concentrates her interactions on the types of things in which her infant has shown an interest.

The latter alternative does, however, seem unlikely in the early months of life, given what we know of the phases of primary and secondary intersubjectivity (Trevarthen, 1979) through which the infant passes. Infants up to around 6 months of age appear to prefer interacting with people to other kinds of activity (primary intersubjectivity), at which point they tend to show a shift in attention towards the object world, assisted by their greater dexterity and increasing cognitive ability (Trevarthen, 1979; Vedeler, 1994). At around 9 months of age, these two systems of interaction come together, and infants now become able to engage in social interactions which involve objects (secondary intersubjectivity).

This shift in infants' attention from the social world to the object world may give us some clues about why a relationship between object-centred interaction and security of attachment has been observed. As discussed in previous chapters, mothers of securely attached children are more sensitive to their children's desires and needs (e.g. Ainsworth et al., 1971; Isabella, 1993); this sensitivity may thus enable them to identify more accurately the point at which their infants start to become interested in objects. Consequently, the relationship between security of attachment and object-centred interaction during the first year of life may be more complex than it initially appears. Indeed, the mother's focus on objects during the phase of primary intersubjectivity may betray a lack of sensitivity to cues from the infant more characteristic of mothers whose children are insecurely attached. One might instead predict that mothers who focus their interactions with their very young infants predominantly on social types of play, and begin to concentrate on objects only when their infants start to show an interest in the physical environment, will be those who are most sensitive and thus most likely to form a secure attachment relationship. We should now turn to a consideration of maternal qualities which may affect the mother's sensitivity to the interests of her child.

Mind-mindedness

I have suggested that one of the most important factors in mothers' ability to interact with their children in a sensitive way is their greater mind-mindedness, or proclivity to treat their infants as individuals with minds. The results of several studies appear to suggest that mothers of securely attached children show greater mind-mindedness. For example, Ainsworth et al. (1971) stated that the mother of a securely attached child is "capable of perceiving things from [the child's] point of view" and treats her child as a "separate person" (p.43). The results of Study Two (see Chapter Four) are also suggestive of such a link. Study Two showed that mothers in the secure group were more likely to attribute meaning to their children's early utterances, whereas the insecure group mothers tended to describe their children's language as "gobbledegook" or "double Dutch". Reports of such "vocal but meaning-less" utterances in the insecure group mothers is consistent with the contention that they are less likely to treat their infants as mental agents, capable of expressing intention through speech.

Of course, all mothers will eventually come to regard their children's utterances and gestures as being intentional, and thus treat their infants as *intentional* agents. But this does not mean that they are necessarily treating their infants as individuals with minds, or *mental* agents. The former merely indicates that the mother believes her child capable of expressing a desire through a particular mode of communication, but the latter indicates that the mother believes her child to be capable of having representations of the world and the different stances that may be taken towards reality. Such a distinction between intentional agency and mental agency has been made by Tomasello, Kruger, and Ratner (1993), who proposed that children are able to understand other people as intentional agents at around 9 months of age, but do not regard others as mental agents until the age of 4 years. But regardless of whether children are able to understand themselves and others as mental agents, caregivers may treat children *as if* they were capable of experiencing such states of mind. Consequently, while maternal mind-mindedness can be seen to result in greater maternal sensitivity to the infant's desires and intentions, it may also have a second function: by treating their infants as individuals with minds, mothers may actually be encouraging their children to understand themselves and others as mental agents. Maternal mind-mindedness may thus be related to the child's self-efficacy, which is a characteristic of securely attached children (see pp.37 and 54–55).

Although considerably more research is needed in this area, there is already some evidence to support a link between maternal mind-mindedness and security of attachment. Meins et al. (in press) found that, when asked to describe their 3-year-old children, mothers in the secure group were more likely than their counterparts in the insecure group to focus on their children's mental attributes, rather than their behavioural tendencies or physical appearance. For example, mothers in the secure group would describe their children as showing "respect for others" and having "minds of their own". We argued that this was evidence for the secure group mothers' propensity to treat their children as mental agents. Moreover, the results of this study can address the suggestion that maternal mind-mindedness is related to children's subsequent ability to understand other people's mental states. These children were followed up at age 4, when they were given a version of the unexpected transfer task (Wimmer & Perner, 1983), which measures children's ability to understand how people's actions are governed by their beliefs about reality, rather than by reality itself (see Study Five). Children whose mothers had described them in mentalistic terms at age 3 were more likely to pass this task at age 4. This suggests that children whose mothers focus on their mental characteristics are subsequently more likely to show an understanding of other people's mental states.

Although these results are highly suggestive of a link between maternal mind-mindedness, security of attachment and children's understanding of other minds, maternal mind-mindedness was not measured until these children were 3 years of age. However, in the preceding discussion on this topic, I have focused on the importance of mind-mindedness in the first year of life, and as yet we do not know whether such early individual differences in maternal mind-mindedness predict subsequent security of attachment, or indeed, whether such early differences exist. In order to address this question, a study is currently underway using a sample of mothers and their 6-month-old infants. The prediction is that differences in mind-mindedness observed at 6 months (such as the mother's willingness to attribute intentionality and meaning to infant actions and vocalisations) will be related to these children's subsequent security of attachment at 12 months. Follow-up studies on this group of children using mentalising tasks (such as those used in Study Five) are planned for the future. This research will provide a unique opportunity to establish the precise links between early maternal mind-mindedness, security of attachment and children's understanding of other minds in early childhood.

Child characteristics: A testing ground for the Vygotskian approach

I stated above that the qualities which the infant brings to the attachment relationship are relatively unimportant when compared with the caregiver's characteristics and the mode of infant-caregiver interaction. In support of this view, I discussed in Chapter Two how under normal circumstances, security of attachment appears not to be greatly affected by infant temperament (e.g. Vaughn et al., 1989). However, more serious individual differences, such as congenital impairment, are bound to have an effect on the emerging attachment relationship. Indeed, this area of research would appear to represent a testing ground for a Vygotskian approach to attachment. I have argued that the caregiver's propensity to treat her infant as an individual with a mind, using feedback from the infant and providing readily assimilable perspectives on the world, are all important factors in the establishment of a secure attachment relationship. It seems likely that a congenital impairment will disrupt these patterns of infant-mother interaction, which may result in problems for the formation of a secure attachment relationship.

Greenberg and Marvin (1979) found that deafness did not automatically cause problems in establishing a secure attachment; rather, it was the effect on mother-child *communication* that appeared to be the crucial factor. Children and mothers who communicated poorly were more likely to show delayed and insecure attachments. In a similar vein, Meadow, Greenberg, and Erting (1985) found that the proportion of secure attachment classifications in deaf children whose parents were also deaf was comparable with that in hearing children. These results underline the importance of intersubjective communication in establishing a secure attachment relationship, suggesting that once mothers have learnt to achieve this by means which do not rely on vocalisation, early disadvantages can be overcome.

Of equal interest in this respect is work done on security of attachment in autistic children. Autistic children have problems with communication and social interaction, and engage in stereotypic or repetitive behaviour (Kanner, 1943; Wing, 1981), all of which would appear to impair their ability to establish relationships with others. Shapiro, Sherman, Calamari, and Koch (1987) and Rogers, Ozonoff, and Maslin-Cole (1991) investigated whether autistic children were able to form secure attachment relationships with their primary caregivers. Both studies reported that autistic children form attachments, and in fact secure attachment behaviour was by no means unusual. Shapiro et al., for example, found that 47% of the autistic children in their sample showed secure attachment behaviour.

At first glance, these findings would appear to present problems for a Vygotskian account of attachment, given autistic individuals' characteristic difficulties in the areas of communication, social interaction and the understanding of other minds (e.g. Baron-Cohen, 1995; Kanner, 1943). But a closer inspection of the literature may help to resolve this puzzle, and perhaps even give us some clues about the factors which predate a secure attachment relationship. Capps, Sigman, and Mundy (1994) investigated the relationship between autism and security of attachment, and additionally employed various measures of language competence and communicative interaction. They reported that those autistic children who demonstrated secure behaviours scored more highly on language comprehension and expression scales, and more frequently used looking, pointing and giving to obtain assistance from their mothers in joint-attentional exchanges. Moreover, these children were more responsive to an experimenter's bids for joint attention, showing a greater use of eye contact and gesture to request objects. This study thus replicated Bretherton et al.'s (1979) findings in an autistic sample of children, further underlining the importance of declarative gestures in the establishment of a secure attachment relationship.

Clearly, these results should not be taken to suggest that the types of relationship which autistic children can establish with their caregivers are identical to those of non-autistic children. Indeed, in Capps et al.'s (1994) study, all of the autistic children were given a primary classification of type D attachment. When a type D attachment classification is given, a secondary classification using Ainsworth et al.'s (1978) three original categories (secure, insecure-avoidant, insecure-resistant) is also made (see p.22), and it was only on this secondary classification that the relationships discussed were found. Nevertheless, although the classic impairments of autism will mean that autistic children's attachment relationships will always be different from those in non-autistic samples, this work shows that autistic children are still capable of forming attachment relationships with their caregivers. More importantly, this research highlights the variation in autistic children's abilities to engage in responsive, intersubjective communication, which suggests that more needs to be done to address the question of individual differences within the autistic population, and thus to move away from the assumption that all autistic children are similarly impaired.

In addressing the question of individual differences in autism, a number of areas appear worthy of investigation. For example, is autistic children's development in the first year of life related to their propensity to show secure attachment behaviour? Some parents report that they were aware of their child having problems in relating to others practically from birth; other parents report that their child appeared to be developing normally up to the age of around 18 months, at which point problems in communication and social interaction began. While there are obvious problems relating to retrospective reporting, such differences in early development are a possibility. It may be that those autistic children who show secure attachment behaviour were those who appeared to be developing normally in the first year of life. The fact that autistic children are apparently capable of demonstrating secure attachment behaviour also raises an interesting question in relation to their subsequent ability to understand other minds. The results of Study Five showed that securely attached children were more likely than their insecurely attached peers to pass a version of the unexpected transfer task (Wimmer & Perner, 1983). Baron-Cohen et al. (1985) reported that around 80% of autistic children fail the unexpected transfer task. Researchers have tended to focus on the majority of autistic children who fail, but what of the substantial minority who pass this task? It may be that this minority represent those children who experienced relatively normal early patterns of interaction with their parents, and were more likely to have shown secure attachment behaviour. The research on security of attachment in autistic children thus raises fascinating questions which are worthy of future investigation.

Evidence from autistic individuals appears to support a Vygotskian approach to mentalising abilities, but once again other congenital impairments would provide a testing ground for this theory. Specifically, a priority should be given to comparing congenitally deaf and blind children of hearing and sighted parents with deaf and blind children whose parents share their impairment. The prediction from the Vygotskian account would be that congenitally impaired children whose primary caregiver shares their impairment will be less delayed in acquiring mentalising abilities, since fewer problems will be encountered in establishing intersubjective patterns of communication and interaction. Indirect support for this prediction, given the proposed link between secure attachment and mentalising abilities, is provided by the finding that the rates of secure attachment relationships in deaf children of deaf parents are comparable with those in the hearing population (Meadow et al., 1985). In addition, we already know that deaf (Peterson & Siegal, 1995) and blind (Minter, Hobson, & Bishop, in press) children perform comparatively poorly on mentalising tasks. However, research has yet to address whether children who are born to parents who share their impairment will be at a relative advantage on tasks of this sort. The abilities of these different groups within the congenitally blind and deaf populations should also be compared with sighted and hearing children to establish whether any attendant deficits are related to the impairment *per se*, or to the problems in communication and intersubjectivity between caregiver and child that such impairments may cause.

BEYOND THE VYGOTSKIAN APPROACH

A Vygotskian approach both to the development of a secure attachment relationship and to children's understanding of other minds is not inconsistent with the existing data. As already discussed, maternal mind-mindedness can go some way to providing an explanation of how some mothers are sensitive to their children's ZPD and thus pitch their interactions accordingly. In turn, one can see how this process nurtures the child's sense of self-efficacy, in that interactions within the ZPD are aimed at a level slightly above the child's current understanding, thus encouraging the child to take on greater responsibility within the interaction. Maternal mind-mindedness can also explain why sensitive maternal interaction, associated with secure attachment, is related to children's subsequent understanding of other minds. By focusing on young children as individuals with minds, caregivers may nurture their children's developing understanding of themselves and others as mental agents.

However, the concepts on which this Vygotskian approach is founded, such as the ZPD, are somewhat vague. One major shortcoming of Vygotsky's theory is that he did not discuss whether the regularity or consistency of interaction within the ZPD affected the internalisation process, and thus the development of the higher mental functions. This point brings me back to the notion of sensitive dyadic interaction providing the child with a "template" for interacting with others (see pp.90 and 109). It seems likely that such a template will only be developed if the caregiver's mode of interaction with the child is consistent. It does not follow, however, that consistent interactions always fall within the ZPD. For example, one could argue that the type of interaction experienced by securely attached children will enable them to develop: (1) a sense of self-efficacy and understanding of themselves and others as mental agents via their mothers' greater mind-mindedness and ability to focus on their ZPD; and (2) a template for interacting with others because of their mothers' consistent mode of interaction. It may be that this distinction between *sensitive* interaction and *consistent* interaction can highlight potential differences between the three insecure attachment groups.

We know from previous research that mothers of insecure-avoidant infants are consistently rejecting in the first year of life (Ainsworth, 1982; Isabella, 1993), whereas mothers of insecure-resistant infants show inconsistent patterns of mothering (Isabella, 1993; Isabella & Belsky, 1991). If one of the reasons why dyadic interaction is important for the child's subsequent development is because it provides the child with a template for interacting with others, it may be that insecure-avoidant children will be at an advantage over their insecure-resistant peers. Even though the avoidant children's mothers have not pitched their interactions within the ZPD, they have at least been consistent in their mode of behaviour, which may allow these children to make predictions about how future interactions will progress, and perhaps use this as a template for interacting with others. If sensitive interactions and consistency in the mode of interaction have an additive effect on the child's development, one would predict that, on any given task, securely attached children will perform best, followed by insecure-avoidant children, with insecure-resistant children performing worst. As far as the insecure-disorganised group are concerned, it is difficult to make any clear predictions, especially if the type D classification is related to abuse or maternal depression. But perhaps even unipolar depression and abuse enable the child to make predictions about how their caregiver will interact with them, and thus provide them with a template for interacting with others.

Clearly, these points are speculative, and a priority should be given to investigating the role played by consistent non-ZPD interaction in the child's development of the higher mental functions, specifically in relation to the three insecure patterns of attachment. Such research would help us to clarify whether one of the reasons why ZPD interaction is important in this process relates to consistency in the mode of dyadic interaction.

IMPLICATIONS FOR FUTURE DEVELOPMENT

I have suggested that experience of early interactions in which the mother demonstrates mind-mindedness may be an important precursor of a secure attachment, which in turn affects the child's understanding of mental states. As well as investigating the establishment of the attachment relationship in the first year of life, it is equally important to chart the progress and development of securely and insecurely attached children as they get older. Since securely attached children appear to have a greater sense of themselves and others as mental agents, will these advantages in childhood persist into adolescence and adulthood? Long-term longitudinal studies, of the sort being carried out by the Grossmanns in Germany, are addressing some of these questions by following up infants into late childhood and adolescence. Such work may eventually enable us to establish whether infantile security of attachment affects individuals' attachment relationships with children of their own. We already know from the work of Fonagy and his colleagues that a mother's classification on the Adult Attachment Interview (AAI) is related to her child's subsequent security of attachment. For example, Fonagy et al. (1991) found that mothers who had resolved any difficulties from their own childhoods tended to have securely attached children. This process of resolution seemed to depend upon a woman's greater willingness to understand the reasons behind the actions of others, and to try to tap into the mind governing the behaviour. This enabled her to be aware "of the multiple motives ... that guided her parents' behaviour toward her" (Fonagy et al., 1991, p.901). It is interesting to note that this process bears a distinct resemblance to the characteristic patterns of interaction between the secure infant and mother within the ZPD. Mothers of securely attached children appear better able to "tune in" to what is going on in their children's minds and pitch their interventions accordingly.

The parents who are perhaps most interesting are those who have "earned" their autonomous, secure rating on the AAI (see p.35). One could argue that this group will be the most likely to have secure attachment relationships with their own children because, in overcoming their own difficult childhood experiences, they will have had to consider and evaluate exactly what types of parent-child interaction constitute good parenting. Once again, this is an interesting question which deserves further investigation, but there is some indirect evidence which appears to support this contention. Several authors have investigated intergenerational transfer of abuse, whereby an abused child becomes an abusing adult (e.g. Egeland, Jacobvitz, & Papatola, 1988), and the factors which may be important in breaking this cycle. It would appear that individuals who have been able to understand the reasons behind the abusive behaviour are less likely to become abusers themselves. For example, Egeland, Jacobvitz, and Sroufe (1988) found that the presence of a caring, non-abusing adult to whom the child could turn at the time of the abuse, along with subsequent counselling and the establishment of a confiding relationship with a partner, could all break the intergenerational cycle of abuse. One might argue that all of these factors have allowed the abused individual to make an attempt to understand and come to terms with what happened to them in childhood. To put it another way, looking to the mental states governing their abuser's words and actions may provide abused individuals with greater understanding, which in turn may lead to resolution and the breaking of the abusive cycle.

These findings on the role played by other adults in children's development illustrate the restrictions of focusing only on attachment relationships with caregivers. Children grow up in families and form friendships, and the importance of interactions with people other than primary caregivers should not be overlooked. One should bear in mind Bowlby's words: "[h]uman personality is perhaps the most complex of all complex systems here on earth. To describe the principal components of its construction, to understand and predict the ways in which it works and ... to map the multitude of intricate paths along any of which one person may develop, these are all tasks for the future" (1973, p.419). But with patient, longitudinal work these important questions can be answered. This kind of research may thus establish whether the effects of childhood security of attachment are fundamental, and provide future generations with a basis for understanding the importance of mental agency in development throughout the life course.

NOTE

1. The data collected in the five studies reported here all refer to the same group of children, using security of attachment as the major independent variable. For completeness, it is worthwhile to indicate how the different measures taken over the four-year period of the longitudinal study relate to one another. Appendix 1 shows the correlation matrix for all of the major variables measured in the five studies.

APPENDIX 1

Correlations between measures from Studies One to Five

	Sec	Ref	FP	VBM	Ex	MS	UTT	PI	FBE	BPVS
Sec	1.00									
Ref	0.79††	1.00								
FP	-0.69††	-0.67††	1.00							
VBM	-0.66††	-0.54†	0.49†	1.00						
Ex	0.63††	0.53††	-0.42**	-0.51††	1.00					
MS	0.55†	0.43**	-0.40**	-0.30*	0.46**	1.00				
UTT	0.51**	0.77††	-0.59†	-0.52**	0.55**	0.42*	1.00			
PI	0.40*	0.40*	-0.42*	-0.22	0.13	0.16	0.27	1.00		
FBE	0.23	0.20	-0.11	-0.35*	0.16	0.29	0.41*	0.11	1.00	
BPVS	0.09	0.18	-0.10	-0.16	0.43*	0.09	0.47*	0.20	-0.22	1.00

Note: Sec = security of attachment; Ref = proportion of common nouns in first 25 words; FP = frozen phrases; VBM = vocal but meaningless utterances; Ex = executive capacity; MS = maternal sensitivity; UTT = unexpected transfer task; PI = picture identification task; FBE = false belief and emotion task; BPVS = British Picture Vocabulary Scale.

$*p < 0.05; **p < 0.005; †p < 0.025; ††p < 0.001$. Significance levels are for one-tailed tests, *except* those involving the BPVS (two-tailed).

References

Ainsworth, M. D. (1963). The development of infant-mother interaction among the Ganda. In B. M. Foss (Ed.), *Determinants of infant behaviour* (Vol. 2). London: Methuen; New York: Wiley.

Ainsworth, M. D. S. (1967). *Infancy in Uganda: Infant care and the growth of love*. Baltimore: Johns Hopkins University Press.

Ainsworth, M. D. S. (1972). Attachment and dependency: A comparison. In J. L. Gewirtz (Ed.), *Attachment and dependency*. Washington DC: Winston.

Ainsworth, M. D. S. (1973). The development of infant-mother attachment. In B. M. Cauldwel & H. N. Ricciuti (Eds.), *Review of child development research* (Vol. 3). Chicago: University of Chicago Press.

Ainsworth, M. D. S. (1982). Attachment: retrospect and prospect. In C. M. Parkes & J. Stevenson-Hinde (Eds.), *The place of attachment in human behaviour*. New York: Basic Books; London: Tavistock Publications.

Ainsworth, M. D. S. (1995). On the shaping of attachment theory and research. In E. Waters, B. E. Vaughn, G, Posada, & K. Kondo-Ikemura (Eds.), *Caregiving, cultural, and cognitive perspectives on secure-base behavior and working models. Monographs of the Society for Research in Child Development, 60* (2–3, Serial No. 244).

Ainsworth, M. D. S., Bell, S. M., & Stayton, D. J. (1971). Individual differences in Strange Situation behaviour of one year olds. In H. R. Schaffer (Ed.), *The origins of human social relations*. New York: Academic Press.

Ainsworth, M. D. S., Bell, S. M., & Stayton, D. J. (1974). Infant-mother attachment and social development: Socialisation as a product of reciprocal responsiveness to signals. In M. P. Richards (Ed.), *The introduction of the child into a social world*. London: Cambridge University Press.

Ainsworth, M. D. S., Blehar, M. C., Waters, E., & Wall, S. (1978). *Patterns of attachment: Assessed in the strange situation and at home*. Hillsdale, NJ: Lawrence Erlbaum Associates Inc.

Ainsworth, M. D. S., & Wittig, B. A. (1969). Attachment and exploratory behaviour of one year olds in a strange situation. In B.M. Foss (Ed.), *Determinants of infant behaviour* (Vol. 4). London: Methuen; New York: Barnes and Noble.

Arend, R. Gove, F. L., & Sroufe. L. A. (1979). Continuity of individual adaptation from infancy to kindergarten: A predictive study of ego-resiliency and curiosity in pre-schoolers. *Child Development, 50*, 950–959.

Astington, J. W. (1996). What is theoretical about a child's theory of mind? A Vygotskian view of development. In P. Carruthers & P. K. Smith (Eds.), *Theories of theories of mind*. Cambridge: Cambridge University Press.

Baillargeon, R. (1987). Object permanence in 3.5 and 4.5 month old infants. *Developmental Psychology, 23*, 655–664.

Baillargeon, R. (1991). Reasoning about the height and location of a hidden object in 4.5– and 6.5–month-old infants. *Cognition, 38*, 13–42.

Baillargeon, R. (1994). Physical reasoning in young infants: Seeking explanations for impossible events. *British Journal of Developmental Psychology, 12*, 9–33.

Baillargeon, R., Graber, M., Devos, J., & Black, J. (1990). Why do young infants fail to search for hidden objects? *Cognition, 36*, 255–284.

Barglow, P., Vaughn, B. E., & Molitor, N. (1987). Effects of maternal employment on the quality of infant-mother attachment in a low-risk sample. *Child Development, 58*, 945–954.

Baron-Cohen, S. (1995). *Mindblindness: An essay on autism and theory of mind*. Cambridge, MA: MIT Press.

Baron-Cohen, S., Leslie, A. M., & Frith, U. (1985). Does the autistic child have a 'theory of mind'? *Cognition, 21*, 37–46.

Bartsch, K., & Wellman, H. M. (1989). Young children's attribution of action to beliefs and desires. *Child Development, 60*, 946–964.

Bates, E., Bretherton, I., & Snyder, L. (1988). *From first words to grammar*. Cambridge: Cambridge University Press.

Bates, E., O'Connell, B., & Shore, C. (1987). Language and communication in infancy. In J. D. Osofsky (Ed.), *Handbook of infant development* (2nd ed.). New York: Wiley.

Bates, E. Thal, D, Fenson, L., Whitesell, K., & Oakes, L. (1989). Integrating language and gesture in infancy. *Developmental Psychology, 25*, 1004–1019.

Bee, H. L., van Egeren, L. F., Pytkowicz Streissguth, A., Nyman, B. A., & Leckie, M. S. (1969). Social class differences in maternal teaching strategies and speech patterns. *Developmental Psychology, 1*, 726–734.

Bell, S. M. (1970). The development of the concept of the object and its relationship to infant-mother attachment. *Child Development, 41*, 291–312.

Belsky, J. (1988). The "effects" of infant day care reconsidered. *Early Childhood Research Quarterly, 3*, 235–272.

Belsky, J., Garduque, L., & Hrncir, E. (1984). Assessing performance, competence and executive capacity in infant play: Relations to home environment and security of attachment. *Developmental Psychology, 20*, 406–417.

Belsky, J., Goode, M., & Most, R. (1980). Maternal stimulation and infant exploratory competence: Cross-sectional, correlational and experimental analyses. *Child Development, 51*, 1163–1178.

Belsky, J., & Most, R. K. (1981). From exploration to play: A cross-sectional study of infant free play behavior. *Developmental Psychology, 17*, 630–639.

Belsky, J., & Rovine, M. (1987). Temperament and attachment security in the strange situation: An empirical rapprochement. *Child Development, 58*, 787–795.

Belsky, J., & Rovine, M. (1988). Nonmaternal care in the first year of life and infant-parent attachment security. *Child Development, 59*, 157–167.

Belsky, J., Rovine, M. J., & Taylor, D. G. (1984). The origins of individual differences in infant-mother attachment: Maternal and infant contributions. *Child Development, 55*, 718–728.

Benedek, T. (1956). Toward the biology of the depressive constellation. *Journal of the American Psychoanalytic Association, 4*, 389–427.

Bernstein, B. (1961). Social class and linguistic development: A theory of social learning. In A. H. Halsey, J. Floud, & C. A., Anderson (Eds.), *Education, economy and society*. New York: Free Press.

Block, J. H., & Block, J. (1980). The role of ego-control and ego-resiliency in the organisation of behaviour. In *Minnesota symposium on child psychology* (Vol. 13, 39–101). Hillsdale, NJ: Lawrence Erlbaum Associates Inc.

Bowlby, J. (1940). The influence of early environment in the development of neurosis and neurotic character. *International Journal of Psycho-Ananlysis, 21*, 1–25.

Bowlby, J. (1951). *Maternal care and mental health*. Geneva: WHO; London: HMSO; New York: Columbia University Press. Abridged version, *Child care and the growth of love*. Harmondsworth, UK: Penguin Books (2nd ed., 1965).

Bowlby, J. (1958). The nature of the child's tie to his mother. *International Journal of Psycho-Analysis, 39*, 350–73.

Bowlby, J. (1960a). Separation anxiety: A critical review of the literature. *International Journal of Psycho-Analysis, 41*, 251–269.

Bowlby, J. (1960b). Grief and mourning in infancy and early childhood. *Psychoanalytic Study of the Child, 15*, 9–52.

Bowlby, J. (1969). *Attachment and Loss: Vol. 1 - Attachment*. London: Hogarth Press.

Bowlby, J. (1973). *Attachment and Loss: Vol. 2 - Separation*. London: Hogarth Press.

Bowlby, J. (1980). *Attachment and Loss: Vol. 3 - Loss*. London: Hogarth Press.

Bowlby, J. (1988). Developmental psychiatry comes of age. *The American Journal of Psychiatry, 145*, 1–10.

Bretherton, I. (1980). Young children in stressful situations: The supporting role of attachment figures and unfamiliar caregivers. In G. V. Coelho & P. Ahmed (Eds.), *Uprooting and development*. New York: Plenum Press.

Bretherton, I. (1987). New perspectives on attachment relations: Security, communication, and internal working models. In J. Osofsky (Ed.), *Handbook of infant development*. New York: Wiley.

Bretherton, I., Bates, E. Benigni, L., Camaioni, L., & Volterra, V. (1979). Relationships between cognition, communcation, and quality of attachment. In E. Bates (Ed.), *The emergence of symbols: Cognition and communication in infancy*. New York: Academic Press.

Bretherton, I., & Beeghly, M. (1982). Talking about internal states: The acquisition of an explicit theory of mind. *Developmental Psychology, 18,* 906–921.

Brossard, M. D. (1974). The infant's concept of object permanence and his reactions to strangers. In T. G. Décarie (Ed.), *The infant's reaction to strangers.* New York: International Universities Press.

Brown, G. W., & Harris, T. (1978). *Social origins of depression.* London: Tavistock Publications.

Brownell, C. A. (1988). Combinatorial skills: Converging developments over the second year. *Child Development, 59,* 675–685.

Bruner, J. S. (1973). Organization of early skilled action. *Child Development, 44,* 1–11.

Bruner, J. S. (1974). Nature and uses of immaturity. In J. Connolly & J. S. Bruner (Eds.), *The growth of competence.* London: Academic Press.

Bruner, J. S. (1977). Early social interaction and language development. In H. R. Schaffer (Ed.), *Studies in mother-infant interaction.* London: Academic Press.

Burlingham, D., & Freud, A. (1942). *Young children in war-time.* London: Allen and Unwin.

Butterworth, G. (1977). Object disappearance and error in Piaget's stage IV task. *Journal of Experimental Child Psychology, 23,* 391–401.

Capps, L., Sigman, M., & Mundy, P. (1994). Attachment security in children with autism. *Development and Psychopathology, 6,* 249–261.

Carlson, V., Cicchetti, D., Barnett, D., & Braunwald, K. (1989). Disorganized/disoriented attachment relationships in maltreated infants. *Developmental Psychology, 25,* 525–531.

Cicchetti, D. (1990). The organisation and coherence of socioemotional, cognitive, and representational development: Illustration through a developmental psychopathology perspective on Down's syndrome and child maltreatment. In R. Thompson (Ed.), *Socioemotional development. Nebraska Symposium on Motivation.* Lincoln: University of Nebraska Press.

Cicchetti, D., & Barnett, D. (1991). Attachment organization in maltreated preschoolers. *Development and Psychopathology, 3,* 397–411.

Clarke-Stewart, K. (1989). Infant day care: Maligned or malignant? *American Psychologist, 44,* 266–273.

Clinchy, B. (1974). *Recognition and production of information-processing strategies in children.* Unpublished doctoral dissertation, Harvard University.

Connell, D. B. (1976). *Individual differences in attachment: An investigation into stability, implications, and relationships to structure of early language development.* Unpublished doctoral dissertation, Syracuse University.

Crittenden, P. M., & Ainsworth, M. D. S. (1989). Child maltreatment and attachment theory. In D. Cicchetti & V. Carlson (Eds.), *Child maltreatment: Theory and research on the causes and consequences of child abuse and neglect.* Cambridge: Cambridge University Press.

Crockenberg, S. (1981). Infant irritability, mother responsiveness, and social support influences on the security of infant-mother attachment. *Child Development, 52,* 857–865.

Cummings, E. M., & Bjork, E. L. (1983). Search behavior on multi-choice hiding tasks: Evidence for an objective conception of space in infancy. *International Journal of Behavioral Development, 6,* 71–87.

Della Corte, M., Benedict, H., & Klein, D. (1983). The relationship of pragmatic dimensions of mothers' speech to the referential-expressive distinction. *Journal of Child Language, 10*, 35–44.

Diamond, A. (1988). Abilities and neural mechanisms underlying AB performance. *Child Development, 59*, 523–527.

Diamond, A. (1991). Neuropsychological insights into the meaning of object concept development. In S. Carey & R. Gelman (Eds.), *The epigenesis of mind: Essays on biology and knowledge.* Hillsdale, NJ: Lawrence Erlbaum Associates Inc.

Diaz, R. M., Neal, C. J., & Vachio, A. (1991). Maternal teaching strategies in the zone of proximal development: A comparison of low- and high-risk dyads. *Merrill-Palmer Quarterly, 37*, 83–108.

Dunn, J., Brown, J., Slomkowski, C., Tesla, C., & Youngblade, L. M. (1991). Young children's understanding of other people's feelings and beliefs: Individual differences and their antecedents. *Child Development, 62*, 1352–1366.

Dunn, L. M., Dunn, L. M., Whetton, C., & Pintilie, D. (1982). *British Picture Vocabulary Scale.* Windsor, UK: NFER-Nelson.

Durrett, M. E., Otaki, M., & Richards, P. (1984). Attachment and mother's perception of support from the father. *International Journal of Behavioral Development, 7*, 167–176.

Egeland, B., & Farber, E. (1984). Infant-mother attachment: Factors related to its development and change over time. *Child Development, 60*, 753–771.

Egeland, B., Jacobvitz, D., & Papatola, K. (1988). Intergenerational continuity of parental abuse. In J. Lancaster & R. Gelles (Eds.), *Biosocial aspects of child abuse.* New York: Jossey-Bass.

Egeland, B., Jacobvitz, D., & Sroufe, L. A. (1988). Breaking the cycle of abuse. *Child Development, 59*, 1080–1088.

Egeland, B., & Sroufe, L. A. (1981). Attachment and early maltreatment. *Child Development, 52*, 44–52.

Elliot, C. D., Murray, D. J., & Pearson, L. S. (1983). *British Ability Scales.* Windsor, UK: NFER- Nelson.

Fernyhough, C. (1994). *Social and private speech as determinants of early cognitive functioning.* Unpublished doctoral dissertation, University of Cambridge.

Fernyhough, C. (1996). The dialogic mind: A dialogic approach to the higher mental functions. *New Ideas in Psychology, 14*, 47–62.

Fernyhough, C. (in press). Vygotsky's sociocultural approach: Theoretical issues and implications for current research. In S. Hala (Ed.), *The development of social cognition.* Hove, UK: Psychology Press.

Flavell, J. H. (1985). *Cognitive development* (2nd ed.). Englewood Cliffs, NJ: Prentice-Hall.

Flavell, J. H., Everett, B. A., Croft, K., & Flavell, E. R. (1981). Young children's knowledge about visual perception: Further evidence for the Level 1–Level 2 distinction. *Developmental Psychology, 17*, 99–103.

Fonagy, P., Redfern, S., & Charman, A. (1997). The relationship between belief-desire reasoning and a projective measure of attachment security (SAT). *British Journal of Developmental Psychology, 15*, 51–63.

Fonagy, P., Steele, M., Moran, G. S., Steele, H., & Higgitt, A. C. (1991). The capacity for understanding mental states: The reflective self in parent and child and its significance for security of attachment. *Infant Mental Health Journal, 13,* 200–216.

Fonagy, P., Steele, H., & Steele, M. (1991). Maternal representations of attachment during pregnancy predict the organisation of infant-mother attachment at one year of age. *Child Development, 62,* 891–905.

Fonagy, P., Steele, M., Steele, H., Higgitt, A. C., & Target, M. (1994). The Emmanuel Miller Memorial Lecture 1992: The theory and practice of resilience. *Journal of Child Psychology and Psychiatry, 35,* 231–257.

Fox, N. A., Kimmerly, N. L., & Schafer, W. D. (1991). Attachment to mother/attachment to father: A meta-analysis. *Child Development, 62,* 210–225.

Frankel, K. A., & Bates, J. E. (1990). Mother-toddler problem solving: Antecedents in attachment, home behavior, and temperament. *Child Development, 61,* 810–819.

Freud, A., & Dann, S. (1951). An experiment in group upbringing. *Psychoanalytic Study of the Child, 6,* 127–168.

Freud, S. (1894). *The neuropsychoses of defence. S. E., 3.* London: Hogarth Press.

Freud, S. (1931). *Female sexuality. S. E., 21.* London: Hogarth Press.

Freud, S. (1939). *Moses and monotheism. S. E. 23.* London: Hogarth Press.

Freud, S. (1940). *An outline of psycho-analysis. S. E. 23.* London: Hogarth Press.

Furrow, D., & Nelson, K. (1984). Environmental correlates of individual differences in language acquisition. *Journal of Child Language, 11,* 523–534.

George, C., Kaplan, N., & Main, M. (1985). *The Adult Attachment Interview.* Unpublished manuscript. University of California at Berkeley.

Gersten, M., Coster, W., Schneider-Rosen, K., Carlson, V., & Cicchetti, D. (1986). The socio-emotional bases of communicative functioning: Quality of attachment, language development, and early maltreatment. In M. Lamb, A. L. Brown, & B. Rogoff (Eds.), *Advances in developmental psychology* (Vol. 4). Hillsdale NJ: Lawrence Erlbaum Associates Inc.

Goldfield, B. A. (1985). *The contribution of child and caregiver to referential and expressive language.* Unpublished doctoral dissertation, Harvard University.

Goldfield, B. A. (1986). Referential and expressive language: a study of two mother-child dyads. *First Language, 6,* 119–131.

Goldfield, B. A., & Reznick, J. S. (1990). Early lexical acquisition: Rate, content and the vocabulary spurt. *Journal of Child Language, 17,* 171–183.

Goldsmith, H. H., & Campos, J. J. (1982) Toward a theory of infant temperament. In R. N. Emde & R. J. Harmon (Eds.), *The development of attachment and affiliative systems.* New York: Plenum Press.

Goosens, F. A., & van IJzendoorn, M. H. (1990). Quality of infants' attachment to professional caregivers: Relation to infant-parent attachment and day-care characteristics. *Child Development, 61,* 832–837.

Gopnik, A. (1988). Conceptual and semantic development as theory change: The case of object permanence. *Mind and Language, 3,* 197–216.

Gopnik, A., & Astington, J. W. (1988). Children's understanding of representational change and its relation to the understanding of false belief and the appearance-reality distinction. *Child Development, 59,* 26–37.

Gopnik, A., & Meltzoff, A. N. (1985). Words, plans, things and locations: Interactions between semantic and cognitive development in the one-word stage. In S. Kuczaj & M. Barrett (Eds.), *The development of word meaning*. New York: Springer-Verlag.

Gopnik, A., & Meltzoff, A. N. (1986). Relations between semantic and cognitive development in the one-word stage: The specificity hypothesis. *Child Development, 57*, 1040–1053.

Gopnik, A., & Meltzoff, A. N. (1987). Early semantic developments and their relationship to object permanence, means-end understanding and categorization. In K. Nelson & A. van Kleeck (Eds.), *Children's language*. Hillsdale, NJ: Lawrence Erlbaum Associates Inc.

Gopnik, A., & Wellman, H. M. (1992). Why the child's theory of mind is really a theory. *Mind and Language, 1*, 158–171.

Goulet, J. (1974) The infant's conception of causality and his reactions to strangers. In T. G. Décarie (Ed.), *The infant's reaction to strangers*. New York: International Universities Press.

Gove, F. (1983). *Patterns and organizations of behavior and affective expression during the second year of life*. Unpublished doctoral dissertation, University of Minnesota.

Greenberg, M., & Marvin, R. (1979). Attachment patterns in profoundly deaf preschool children. *Merrill-Palmer Quarterly, 25*, 265–279.

Grosskurth, P. (1987). *Melanie Klein: Her world and her work*. Cambridge, MA: Harvard University Press.

Grossmann, K. E., Grossmann, K., Huber, F., & Wartner, U. (1981). German children's behaviour towards their mothers at 12 months and their fathers at 18 months in Ainsworth's Strange Situation. *International Journal of Behavioral Development, 4*, 157–181.

Grossmann, K. E., Grossmann, K., Spangler, G., Suess, G., & Unzner, L. (1985). Maternal sensitivity and newborns' orientation responses as related to quality of attachment in northern Germany. In I. Bretherton & E. Waters (Eds.), *Growing points of attachment theory and research. Monographs of the Society for Research in Child Development, 50* (1–2, Serial No. 209).

Harlow, H. F. (1961). The development of affectional patterns in infant monkeys. In B. M. Foss (Ed.), *Determinants of infant behaviour* (Vol. 1). London: Methuen; New York: Wiley.

Harlow, H. F., & Harlow, M. K. (1962). Social deprivation in monkeys. *Scientific American, 207*, 136.

Harris, P. L. (1974). Perseverative search at a visibly empty space in young infants. *Journal of Experimental Child Psychology, 18*, 535–42.

Harris, P. L. (1991). The work of the imagination. In A. Whiten (Ed.), *Natural theories of mind: Evolution, development and simulation of everyday mindreading*. Oxford: Basil Blackwell.

Harris, P. L., Johnson, C. L., Hutton, D., Andrews, G., & Cooke, T. (1989). Young children's theory of mind and emotion. *Cognition and Emotion, 3*, 379–400.

Hazen, N. L., & Durrett, M. E. (1982). Relationship of security of attachment to exploration and cognitive mapping abilities in 2–year-olds. *Developmental Psychology, 18*, 751–759.

Hess, R. D., & Shipman, V. (1965). Early experience and the socialization of cognitive modes in children. *Child Development, 34*, 869–886.

Hobson, R. P. (1989). Beyond cognition: a theory of autism. In G. Dawson (Ed.), *Autism: New perspectives on diagnosis, nature and treatment*. New York: Guilford Press.

Hobson, R. P. (1990). On acquiring knowledge about people and the capacity to pretend: Response to Leslie (1987). *Psychological Review, 97*, 114–121.

Hobson, R. P. (1993). *Autism and the development of mind*. Hove, UK: Lawrence Erlbaum Associates Ltd.

Hogrefe, G. J., Wimmer, H., & Perner, J. (1986). Ignorance versus false belief: A developmental lag in attribution of epistemic states. *Child Development, 57*, 567–582.

Horgan, D. (1979). *Nouns: Love 'em or leave 'em*. Address to the New York Academy of Sciences.

Isabella, R. A. (1993). Origins of attachment: Maternal interactive behavior across the first year. *Child Development, 64*, 605–621.

Isabella, R. A., & Belsky, J. (1991). Interactional synchrony and the origins of infant-mother attachment: A replication study. *Child Development, 62*, 373–384.

Jackson, E., Campos, J. J., & Fischer, K. W. (1978). The question of décalage between object permanence and person permanence. *Developmental Psychology, 14*, 1–10.

Jenkins, J. M., & Astington, J. W. (1996). Cognitive factors and family structure associated with theory of mind development in young children. *Developmental Psychology, 32*, 70–78.

Johnson, C. N. (1988). Theory of mind and the structure of conscious experience. In J. W. Astington, P. L. Harris, & D. R. Olson (Eds.), *Developing theories of mind*. Cambridge: Cambridge University Press.

Kagan, J. (1982). *Psychological research on the human infant: An evaluative summary*. New York: William T. Grant Foundation.

Kanner, L. (1943). Autistic disturbances of affective contact. *Nervous Child, 2*, 217–250.

Klagsbrun, M., & Bowlby, J. (1976). Responses to separation from parents: A clinical test for young children. *British Journal of Projective Psychology and Personality Study, 21*, 7–26.

Klein, M. (1957). *Envy and gratitude*. London: Tavistock Publications.

LaFreniere, P. J., & Sroufe, L. A. (1985). Profiles of peer competence in the preschool: Interrelations among measures, influence of social ecology, and relations to attachment history. *Developmental Psychology, 21*, 56–69.

Lamb, M. E. (1978). Qualitative aspects of mother- and father-infant attachments. *Infant Behavior and Development, 1*, 265–276.

Lamb, M. E. (1981). The development of father-infant relationships. In M. E. Lamb (Ed.) *The role of the father in child development*. New York: Wiley.

Lamb, M. E., Gaensbauer, T. J., Malkin, C. M., & Schultz, L. A. (1985). The effects of child maltreatment on security of infant-mother attachment. *Infant Behavior and Development, 8*, 35–45.

Lamb, M. E., Hwang, C. P., Frodi, A., & Frodi, M. (1982). Security of mother- and father-attachment and its relation to sociability with strangers in traditional and nontraditional Swedish families. *Infant Behavior and Development, 5*, 355–367.

Lamb, M. E., Thompson, R. A., Gardner, W. P., Charnov, E. L., & Estes, D. (1984). Security of infantile attachment as assessed in the "strange situation": Its study and biological interpretation. *The Behavioral and Brain Sciences, 7,* 127–171.

Laosa, L. (1980) Maternal teaching strategies in Chicano and Anglo-American families: The influence of culture and education on maternal behavior. *Child Development, 51,* 759–765.

Leekam, R. S., & Perner, J. (1991). Does the autistic child have a metarepresentational deficit? *Cognition, 40,* 203–218.

Lempers, J., Flavell, E., & Flavell, J. H. (1977). The development in very young children of tacit knowledge concerning visual perception. *Genetic Psychology Monographs, 95,* 3–53.

Leonard, L., Schwartz, R., Folger, M., Newhoff, M., & Wilcox, M. (1979). Children's imitations of lexical items. *Child Development, 59,* 19–27.

Leslie, A. M. (1987). Pretense and representation: The origins of 'theory of mind'. *Psychological Review, 94,* 412–426.

Leslie, A. M., & Frith, U. (1988). Autistic children's understanding of seeing, knowing and believing. *British Journal of Developmental Psychology, 6,* 315–324.

Leslie, A. M., & Frith, U. (1990). Prospects for a cognitive neuropsychology of autism: Hobson's choice. *Psychological Review, 97,* 122–131.

Levine, L. V., Tuber, S. B., Slade, H., & Ward, M. J. (1991). Mothers' mental representations and their relationship to mother-infant attachment. *Bulletin of the Menninger Clinic, 55,* 454–469.

Levitt, M., Antonucci, T., & Clark, M. C. (1984). Object-person permanence and attachment: Another look. *Merrill-Palmer Quarterly, 30,* 1, 1–10.

Lewis, C., Freeman, N. H., Kyriakidou, C., Maridaki-Kassotaki, K., & Berridge, D. (1996). Social influences on false belief access: Specific sibling influences or general apprenticeship? *Child Development, 67,* 2930–2948.

Lewis, M., & Feiring, C. (1989). Infant, mother and mother-infant interaction behavior and subsequent attachment. *Child Development, 60,* 831–837.

Lewis, V., & Boucher, J. (1988). Spontaneous, instructed and elicited play in relatively able autistic children. *British Journal of Developmental Psychology, 6,* 325–339.

Lieberman, A. F. (1977). Preschoolers' competence with a peer: Relations with attachment and peer experience. *Child Development, 48,* 1277–1287.

Lieven, E. V. M., Pine, J. M., & Dresner Barnes, H. (1992). Individual differences in early vocabulary development: Redefining the referential-expressive distinction. *Journal of Child Language, 19,* 287–310.

Light, P., & Nix, C. (1983). 'Own' view versus 'good' view in a perspective-taking task. *Child Development, 54,* 480–483.

Londerville, S., & Main, M. (1981). Security of attachment, compliance, and maternal training methods in the second year of life. *Developmental Psychology, 17,* 289–299.

Lütkenhaus, P., Grossmann, K. E., & Grossmann, K. (1985). Infant-mother attachment at twelve months and style of interaction with a stranger at the age of three years. *Child Development, 56,* 1538–1542.

Main, M. (1973). *Exploration, play, and level of cognitive functioning as related to child-mother attachment.* Unpublished doctoral dissertation, Johns Hopkins University.

Main, M. (1983). Exploration, play, and cognitive functioning as related to infant-mother attachment. *Infant Behavior and Development, 6,* 167–174.

Main, M. (1991). Metacognitive knowledge, metcognitive monitoring, and singular (coherent) vs. multiple (incoherent) model of attachment: Findings and directions for future research. In C. Murray Parkes, J. Stevenson-Hinde, & P. Marris (Eds.), *Attachment across the life cycle.* London: Tavistock.

Main, M., Kaplan, N., & Cassidy, J. (1985). Security in infancy, childhood, and adulthood: A move to the level of representation. In I. Bretherton & E. Waters (Eds.), *Growing points of attachment theory and research. Monographs of the Society for Research in Child Development, 50* (1–2, Serial No. 209).

Main, M., & Solomon, J. (1986). Discovery of a disorganized/disoriented attachment pattern. In T. B. Brazelton & M. W. Yogman (Eds.), *Affective development in infancy.* Norwood, NJ: Ablex.

Main, M., & Weston, D. (1981). The quality of the toddler's relationship to mother and father: related to conflict behaviour and the readiness to establish new relationships. *Child Development, 52,* 932–40.

Main, M., & Weston, D. R. (1982). Avoidance of the attachment figure in infancy: Descriptions and interpretations. In C. M. Parkes & J. Stevenson-Hinde (Eds.), *The place of attachment in human behavior.* New York: Basic.

Matas, L., Arend, R. A., & Sroufe, L. A. (1978). Continuity of adaptation in the second year: The relationship between quality of attachment and later competence. *Child Development, 49,* 547–56.

Mead, G. H. (1934). *Mind, self and society: From the standpoint of a social behaviourist.* Chicago: University of Chicago Press.

Meadow, K. P., Greenberg, M. T., & Erting, C. (1985). Attachment behavior of deaf children of deaf parents. In S. Chess & A. Thomas (Eds.), *Annual progress in child psychiatry and child development.* New York: Brunner/Mazel.

Meins, E. (1997). Security of attachment and maternal tutoring strategies: Interaction within the zone of proximal development. *British Journal of Developmental Psychology, 15,* 129–144.

Meins, E., Fernyhough, C., Russell, J., & Clark-Carter, D. (in press). Security of attachment as a predictor of symbolic and mentalising abilities: A longitudinal study. *Social Development.*

Meins, E., & Russell, J. (1997). Security and symbolic play: The relation between security of attachment and executive capacity. *British Journal of Developmental Psychology, 15,* 63–77.

Milner, B. (1964). Some effects of frontal lobectomy in man. In J. M. Warren & K. Akert (Eds.), *The frontal granular cortex and behavior.* New York: McGraw-Hill.

Minter, M., Hobson, R. P., & Bishop, M. (in press). Congenital visual impairment and 'theory of mind'. *British Journal of Developmental Psychology.*

Miyake, K., Chen, S., & Campos, J. J. (1985). Infant temperament, mother's mode of interaction, and attachment in Japan: An interim report. In I. Bretherton & E. Waters (Eds.), *Growing points of attachment theory and research. Monographs of the Society for Research in Child Development, 50* (1–2, Serial No. 209).

Moore, C., & Frye, D. (1991). The acquisition and utility of theories of mind. In D. Frye & C. Moore (Eds.), *Children's theories of mind: Mental states and social understanding*. Hillsdale, NJ: Lawrence Erlbaum Associates Inc.

Mueller, C. W., & Parcel, T. L. (1981) Measures of socioeconomic status: Alternatives and recommendations. *Child Development, 52,* 13–30.

Murray, L., & Stein, A. (1989). The effects of postnatal depression on the infant. *Bailliere's Clinical Obstetrics and Gynaecology, 3,* 921–933.

Nelson, K. (1973). Structure and strategy in learning to talk. *Monographs of the Society for Research in Child Development, 38,* Nos. 1 & 2.

Nelson, K. (1981). Individual differences in language development: Implications for development and language. *Developmental Psychology, 17,* 170–187.

Nelson, K.E., Baker, N., Denninger, M., Bonvillian, J., and Kaplan, B. (1985). "Cookie" versus "Do-it-again": Imitative-referential and personal-social-syntactic-initiating styles in young children. *Linguistics, 23,* 3.

Newport, E. (1976). Motherese: the speech of mothers to young children. In N. Castellan, D. Pisoni, & G. Potts (Eds.), *Cognitive theory* (Vol. 2). Hillsdale, NJ: Lawrence Erlbaum Associates Inc.

Newport, E., Gleitman, H., & Gleitman, L. (1977). Mother, I'd rather do it myself: Some effects and non-effects of maternal speech style. In C. Snow & C. Ferguson (Eds.), *Talking to children: Language input and acquisition*. Cambridge: Cambridge University Press.

O'Neill, D. K., Astington, J. W., & Flavell, J. H. (1992). Young children's understanding of the role that sensory experiences play in knowledge acquisition. *Child Development, 63,* 474–490.

Offer, D. (1969). *The psychological world of the teenager: A study of normal adolescent boys*. New York: Basic Books.

Olson, D. R. (1966). On conceptual strategies. In J. S. Bruner, R. R. Olver, & P. M. Greenfield (Eds.), *Studies in cognitive growth*. Wiley: New York.

Olson, D. R. (1970). *Cognitive development: The child's acquisition of diagonality*. Academic Press: New York.

Olson, D. R., Astington, J. W., & Harris, P. L. (1988). Introduction. In J. A. Astington, P. L. Harris, & D. R. Olson (Eds.), *Developing theories of mind*. Cambridge: Cambridge University Press.

Paradise, E., & Curcio, F. (1974). The relationship of cognitive and affective behaviours to fear of strangers in male infants. *Developmental Psychology, 10,* 476–483.

Peck, R. F., & Havighurst, R. J. (1960). *The psychology of character development*. New York: Wiley.

Perner, J. (1991). *Understanding the representational mind*. Cambridge, MA: MIT Press.

Perner, J., & Leekam, R. S. (1990). *Children's difficulty with photography versus colour transmission: Zooming in on representation*. Unpublished manuscript. University of Sussex.

Perner, J., Ruffman, T., & Leekam, S. R. (1994). Theory of mind is contagious: You catch it from your sibs. *Child Development, 65,* 1228–1238.

Peters, A. (1977). Language learning strategies: Does the whole equal the sum of the parts? *Language, 53,* 560–573.

Peterson C. C., & Siegal, M. (1995). Deafness, conversation and theory of mind. *Journal of Child Psychology and Psychiatry, 36,* 459–474.

Piaget, J. (1955). *The child's construction of reality.* London: Routledge and Kegan Paul.

Piaget, J. (1962). *Play, dreams and imitation in childhood.* New York: Norton.

Piaget, J., & Inhelder, B. (1956). *The child's conception of space.* London: Routledge and Kegan Paul.

Pine, J. M. (1989). Reevaluating Nelson's referential-expressive distinction. *Proceedings of the Child Language Seminar, Hatfield Polytechnic.*

Pine, J. M. (1990). *Non-referential children: Slow or different?* Paper presented at the Fifth International Congress for the Study of Child Language, Budapest.

Pine, J. M. (1992). The functional basis of referentiality: Evidence from children's spontaneous speech. *First Language, 12,* 39–55.

Posada, G., Gao, Y., Wu, F., Posada, R., Tascon, M., Schölmerich, A., Sagi, A., Kondo-Ikemura, K., Haaland, W., & Synnevaag, B. (1995). The secure-base phenomenon across cultures: Children's behavior, mothers' preferences, and experts' concepts. In E. Waters, B. E. Vaughn, G, Posada, & K. Kondo-Ikemura (Eds.), *Caregiving, cultural, and cognitive perspectives on secure-base behavior and working models. Monographs of the Society for Research in Child Development, 60* (2–3, Serial No. 244).

Premack, D., & Woodruff, G. (1978). Does the chimpanzee have a theory of mind? *Behavioral and Brain Sciences, 4,* 515–526.

Radke-Yarrow, M., McCann, K., DeMulder, E., Belmont, B., Martinez, P., & Richardson, D. T. (1995). Attachment in the context of high-risk conditions. *Development and Psychopathology, 7,* 247–265.

Robertson, J. (1952). Film: *A two-year-old goes to hospital.* London: Tavistock Child Development Research Unit; New York: New York University Film Library.

Robertson, J. (1953). Some responses of young children to loss of maternal care. *Nursing Times, 49,* 382–386.

Rogers, S. J., Ozonoff, S., & Maslin-Cole, C. (1991). A comparative study of attachment behavior in young children with autism or other psychiatric disorders. *Journal of the American Academy of Child Adolescent Psychiatry, 30,* 483–488.

Russell, J. (1996). *Agency: its role in mental development.* Hove, UK: Psychology Press

Sagi, A., van IJzendoorn, M. H., Aviezer, O., Donnell, F., Koren-Karie, N., Joels, T., & Harel, Y. (1995). Attachments in multiple-caregiver and multiple-infant environment: The case of the Israeli Kibbutzim. In E. Waters, B. E. Vaughn, G, Posada, & K. Kondo-Ikemura (Eds.), *Caregiving, cultural, and cognitive perspectives on secure-base behavior and working models. Monographs of the Society for Research in Child Development, 60* (2–3, Serial No. 244).

Schaffer, H. R., & Emerson, P. E. (1964). The development of social attachments in infancy. *Monographs of the Society for Research in Child Development, 29,* 1–77.

Senn, M. J. E. (1977). *Interview with John Bowlby.* Unpublished manuscript, National Library of Medicine, Washington, DC.

Shallice, T. (1988). *From neurophysiology to cognitive structure.* Cambridge: Cambridge University Press.

Shapiro, R., Sherman, M., Calamari, G., & Koch, D. (1987). Attachment in autism and other developmental disorders. *Journal of the American Academy of Child Adolescent Psychiatry, 26*, 485–490.

Shatz, M., Wellman, H., & Silber, S. (1983). The acquisition of mental verbs: A systematic investigation of the first reference to mental state. *Cognition, 14*, 301–321.

Shaw, P. (1989). *Is the deficit in autistic children's theory of mind an artefact?* Unpublished manuscript. Oxford University.

Shore, C. (1986). Combinatorial play, conceptual development and early multi-word speech. *Developmental Psychology, 22*, 184–190.

Slade, A. (1987a). A longitudinal study of maternal involvement and symbolic play during the toddler period. *Child Development, 58*, 367–375.

Slade, A. (1987b). Quality of attachment and early symbolic play. *Developmental Psychology, 23*, 78–85.

Smith, P. B., & Pederson, D. R. (1988). Maternal sensitivity and patterns of infant-mother attachment. *Child Development, 59*, 1097–1101.

Snyder, L. (1978). Communicative and cognitive abilities and disabilities in the sensorimotor period. *Merrill-Palmer Quarterly, 24*, 161–180.

Spitz, R. A. (1960). Discussion of Dr. John Bowlby's paper. *Psychoanalytic Study of the Child, 15*, 85–208.

Sroufe, L. A. (1983). Infant-caregiver attachment and patterns of adaptation in preschool: The roots of maladaptation and competence. In M. Perlmutter (Ed.), *Development and policy concerning children with special needs.* (Minnesota Symposia on Child Psychology, Vol. 16). Hillsdale, NJ: Lawrence Erlbaum Associates Inc.

Sroufe, L. A. (1985). Attachment classification from the perspective of infant-caregiver relationships and infant temperament. *Child Development, 56*, 1–14.

Sroufe, L. A., Fox, N., & Pancake, V. (1983). Attachment and dependency in developmental perspective. *Child Development, 54*, 1615–1627.

Sroufe, L. A., & Waters, E. (1977). Attachment as an organizational construct. *Child Development, 48*, 1184–1199.

Tamis-LeMonda, C. S., & Bornstein, M. H. (1989). Habituation and maternal encouragement of attention in infancy as predictors of toddler language, play, and representational competence. *Child Development, 60*, 738–751.

Tamis-LeMonda, C. S., & Bornstein, M. H. (1990). Language, play, and attention at one year. *Infant Behavior and Development, 14*, 143–162.

Tamis-LeMonda, C. S., & Bornstein, M. H. (1994). Specificity in mother-toddler language-play relations across the second year. *Developmental Psychology, 30*, 283–292.

Taylor, M., Cartwright, B. S., & Bowden, T. (1991). Perspective taking and theory of mind: Do children predict interpretive diversity as a function of differences in observers' knowledge? *Child Development, 62*, 1334–1351.

Thomas, A., & Chess, S. (1977). *Temperament and development.* New York: Brunner/Mazel.

Thomas, A., Chess, S., Birch, H. G. Hertzig, M. E., & Korn, S. (1963). *Behavioral individuality in early childhood.* New York: New York University Press.

Tomasello, M., Kruger, A. C., & Ratner, H. H. (1993). Cultural learning. *Behavioral and Brain Sciences, 16*, 495–552.

Tomasello, M., & Todd, J. (1983). Joint attention and lexical acquisitional style. *First Language, 4*, 197–212.

Tracy, R. L., & Ainsworth, M. D. S. (1981). Maternal affectionate behaviour and infant-mother attachment patterns. *Child Development, 52*, 1341–1343.

Trevarthen, C. (1977). Descriptive analyses of infant communicative behaviour. In H. R. Schaffer (Ed.), *Studies in mother-child interaction*. London: Academic Press.

Trevarthen, C. (1979). Communication and cooperation in early infancy: A description of primary intersubjectivity. In M. Bullowa (Ed.), *Before speech: The beginning of interpersonal communication*. Cambridge: Cambridge University Press.

Turner, P. J. (1993) Attachment to mother and behaviour with adults in preschool. *British Journal of Developmental Psychology, 11*, 75–89.

Ungerer, J. A., & Sigman, M. (1984). The relation of play and sensorimotor behavior to language in the second year. *Child Development, 55*, 1448–1455.

Uzgiris, I. (1976). Organization of sensorimotor intelligence. In M. Lewis (Ed.), *Origins of intelligence*. New York: Plenum Press.

van IJzendoorn, M. H., Dijkstra, J., & Bus, A. G. (1995). Attachment, intelligence, and language: A meta-analysis. *Social Development, 4*, 115–128.

van IJzendoorn, M. H., Kranenburg, M. J., Zwart-Woudstra, H. A., van Busschbach, A. M., & Lambermon, M. W. (1991). Parental attachment and children's socio-emotional development: Some findings on the validity of the Adult Attachment Interview in the Netherlands. *International Journal of Behavioral Development, 14*, 375–394.

Vaughn, B. E., Deane, K. E., & Waters, E. (1985). The impact of out-of-home care on child-mother attachment quality: Another look at some enduring questions. In I. Bretherton & E. Waters (Eds.), *Growing points of attachment theory and research. Monographs of the Society for Research in Child Development, 50* (1–2, Serial No. 209).

Vaughn, B. E., Egeland, B., Sroufe, L. A., & Waters, E. (1979). Individual differences in infant-mother attachment at twelve and eighteen months: Stability and change in families under stress. *Child Development, 50*, 971–975.

Vaughn, B. E., Gove, F. L., & Egeland, B. (1980). The relationship between daycare and quality of infant-mother attachment in an economically disadvantaged population. *Child Development, 51*, 1203–1214.

Vaughn, B. E., Lefever, G. B., Seifer, R., & Barglow, P. (1989). Attachment behavior, attachment security and temperament during infancy. *Child Development, 60*, 728–737.

Vedeler, D. (1994). Infant intentionality as object directedness: A method for observation. *Scandinavian Journal of Psychology, 35*, 343–366.

Vygotsky, L. S. (1933). Play and its role in the mental development of the child. In J. S. Bruner, A. Jolly, & K. Sylva (Eds.), *Play—Its role in development and evolution*. Harmondsworth, UK: Penguin.

Vygotsky, L. S. (1934/86). *Thought and language*. (A. Kozulin, Ed., & trans.). Cambridge, MA: MIT Press.

Vygotsky, L. S. (1956). *Izbrannye psikhologicheskie issledovaniya*. [Selected psychological investigations]. Moscow: Izdatel'stvo Akademii Pedagogischeskikh Nauk.

Vygotsky, L. S. (1978). *Mind in society: The development of higher psychological processes.* M. Cole, V. John-Steiner, S. Scribner, & E. Souberman (Eds.). Cambridge, MA: Harvard University Press.

Vygotsky, L. S. (1981). The genesis of higher mental functions. In J. V. Wertsch (Ed.), *The concept of activity in Soviet psychology.* Armonk, NY: M. E. Sharpe.

Ward, M. J. (1983). *Maternal behavior with firstborns and secondborns: Evidence for consistency in family relations.* Unpublished doctoral dissertation, University of Minnesota.

Ward, M. J., Vaughn, B. E., & Robb, M. D. (1988). Socio-emotional adaptation and infant-mother attachment in siblings: Role of the mother in cross-sibling consistency. *Child Development, 59,* 643–651.

Waters, E. (1987). *Attachment behavior Q-Set* (Revision 3.0). Unpublished instrument. State University of New York at Stony Brook.

Waters, E., & Deane, K. E. (1985). Defining and assessing individual differences in attachment relationships: Q-methodology and the organization of behavior in infancy and early childhood. In I. Bretherton & E. Waters (Eds.), *Growing points of attachment theory and research. Monographs of the Society for Research in Child Development, 50* (1–2, Serial No. 209).

Waters, E., & Sroufe, L. A. (1983). Social competence as a developmental construct. *Developmental Review, 3,* 79–97.

Waters, E., Wippman, J., & Sroufe, L. A. (1979). Attachment, positive affect and competence in the peer group: Two studies in construct validation. *Child Development, 50,* 821–829.

Wellman, H. M. (1990). *The child's theory of mind.* Cambridge MA: MIT Press.

Wellman, H. M. (1991). From desires to beliefs: Acquisition of a theory of mind. In A. Whiten (Ed.), *Natural theories of mind.* Oxford: Basil Blackwell.

Wellman, H. M., & Banerjee, M. (1991). Mind and emotion: Children's understanding of the emotional consequences of beliefs and desires. *British Journal of Developmental Psychology, 9,* 191–224.

Werner, H., & Kaplan, B. (1963). *Symbol formation.* New York: Wiley.

Wertsch, J. V., & Stone, C. A. (1985). The concept of internalization in Vygotsky's account of the genesis of higher mental functions. In J. V. Wertsch (Ed.), *Culture, communcation and cognition: Vygotskian perspectives.* Cambridge: Cambridge University Press.

Wimmer, H., & Perner, J. (1983). Beliefs about beliefs: Representation and constraining function of wrong beliefs in young children's understanding of deception. *Cognition, 13,* 103–128.

Wimmer, H., & Hartl, M. (1991). Against the Cartesian view on mind: Young children's difficulties with own false beliefs. *British Journal of Developmental Psychology, 9,* 125–138.

Wing, L. (1981). Language, social and cognitive impairments in autism and severe mental retardation. *Journal of Autism and Developmental Disorders, 11,* 31–44.

Wood, D. J., Bruner, J. S., & Ross, G. (1976). The role of tutoring in problem solving. *Journal of Child Psychology and Psychiatry, 17,* 89–100.

Wood, D. J., & Middleton, D. (1975). A study of assisted problem-solving. *British Journal of Psychology, 66,* 181–191.

Wood, D. J., Wood, H. A., & Middleton, D. J. (1978). An experimental evaluation of four face-to-face teaching strategies. *International Journal of Behavioral Development, 1,* 131–147.

Zaitchik,   D. (1990). When representations conflict with reality: The
preschooler's problem with false beliefs and 'false' photographs. *Cognition,*
35, 41–68.

Author index

Subject index

A not B error 42, 43, 45, 51, 53, 54
  see also Piaget's theory
  memory hypothesis 46
  inhibition of prepotent
    responses 46, 47
Abuse 25, 26, 35, 98, 146 *see also*
  Intergenerational transfer
Accommodation 41 *see also* Piaget's
  theory
Adult Attachment Interview 34, 35,
  36, 119, 146
  reflective self scale 118
  earned autonomous 36, 147
Assimilation 41 *see also* Piaget's
  theory
Attachment *see also*
  Avoidance/insecure-avoidant;
  Bowlby's theory;
  Disorganisation/insecure-
  disorganised;
  Resistance/insecure-resistant;
  Security/secure attachment
    and cognitive ability 29, 30, 124,
    125, 128, 133, 134, 136
    distribution across ABC
    categories 30

environmental influences
  30-32
multiple 8
Attachment Q-sort 23
Autism 142, 143, 144
Autonomy 23, 28, 29, 37, 55, 57, 58,
  62, 63, 71, 72, 73, 78, 104 *see also*
  Self-efficacy
Avoidance/insecure-avoidant 3, 10,
  19, 20, 21, 24, 25, 26, 30, 31, 48,
  51, 63, 65, 79, 82, 85, 87, 99, 103,
  107, 120, 123, 124, 138, 143, 145

Blindness 144 *see also* Congenital
  impairment
  and theory of mind
    understanding 144
Bowlby's theory 3, 4, 12, 13, 14, 17,
  18, 19, 33, 40, 129, 130, 135, 147
  see also Freud's theory;
  Goal-corrected system;
  Intergenerational transfer;
  Monotropy; Vygotsky's theory;
  Working models
    attachment theory (1958) 4-7
    attachment theory (1969) 7-9